# Social Workers and Child Abuse Reporting:

## A Review of State Mandatory Reporting Requirements

NASW PRESS

*National Association of Social Workers*
*Washington, DC*

Jeane W. Anastas, PhD, LMSW, *President*
Elizabeth J. Clark, PhD, ACSW, MPH, *Executive Director*

# Social Workers and Child Abuse Reporting: A Review of State Mandatory Reporting Requirements

**General Counsel Law Note**

Carolyn I. Polowy, JD
*NASW General Counsel*

Sherri Morgan, MSW, JD
*NASW Associate General Counsel
LDF and Office of Ethics & Professional Review*

Amber Khan, MA, JD
*Legal Researcher*

Brian W. Schoeneman, MA
*Law Clerk*

Peter McLeod
*Law Clerk (2000 Edition)*

**NASW · LDF**
National Association of Social Workers
Legal Defense Fund

**NASW Press**

Cheryl Y. Bradley
*Publisher*

John Cassels
*Editor*

*This project was funded in part by the Aileen Neely bequest to the NASW Legal Defense Fund.*

©2012 National Association of Social Workers. All Rights Reserved.

# Table of Contents

**Introduction** .................................................. 1

**Federal Legislation—The Child Abuse Prevention and Treatment Act of 1974 (CAPTA)** ............... 3
    **CAPTA Requirements** ............................... 4
    **Minimum Acceptable Definitions** .................... 4

**State Statutes** ................................................ 7
    **Definitions** ............................................. 7
        Child ................................................ 8
        Physical Abuse ..................................... 8
        Sexual Abuse ....................................... 9
        Neglect ............................................. 10
        Emotional Maltreatment ........................... 10
        Corporal Punishment .............................. 10
    **Problems of Ambiguity in State Definitions** ......... 11

**Mandated Reporters** ......................................... 13

**Reporting and Reporting Procedures** ..................... 15
    **Jurisdiction** ............................................ 16
    **Acceptable Time Frame for Reporting** .............. 16
    **Content of Reports** .................................. 16
    **When Reporting Responsibility Ends** ................ 17
    **Privileged Communication Exception** ............... 17

**Immunity** .................................................... 19
    **Good Faith Requirement** ............................ 19
    **Good Faith Presumption** ............................. 20
    **Absolute Immunity** ................................... 20

## Failure to Report . . . . . . . . . . . . . . . . . . . . . . . . . . . . 21
### Criminal Liability . . . . . . . . . . . . . . . . . . . . . . . . . 21
### Civil Liability . . . . . . . . . . . . . . . . . . . . . . . . . . . . 21
### Statutory Civil Liability . . . . . . . . . . . . . . . . . . . . . 22
### Negligence Per Se . . . . . . . . . . . . . . . . . . . . . . . . 23
### General Common Law Tort Theory . . . . . . . . . . . . . . 23
### Professional Malpractice . . . . . . . . . . . . . . . . . . . . . 24
### Intentional False Reporting . . . . . . . . . . . . . . . . . . 24

## Ethical Considerations . . . . . . . . . . . . . . . . . . . . . . . . 27

## Issues Involving CPS Workers . . . . . . . . . . . . . . . . . . 29

## Emerging Issues . . . . . . . . . . . . . . . . . . . . . . . . . . . . 33
### Adult Survivors of Abuse and Adult Recovered Memory . . . . . . . . . . . . . . . . . . . . . . 33
### Cross-Jurisdictional Cases . . . . . . . . . . . . . . . . . . . . 34
### Child Pornography . . . . . . . . . . . . . . . . . . . . . . . . 35
### "Sexting" . . . . . . . . . . . . . . . . . . . . . . . . . . . . . . . 37

## Practical Steps for the Social Worker . . . . . . . . . . . . . 41
### Verify Reporting Duty with Local Authorities . . . . . . . . 41
### Understand the Signs of Abuse . . . . . . . . . . . . . . . . 41
### Understand the Process of Investigation . . . . . . . . . . 41
### Document the Details . . . . . . . . . . . . . . . . . . . . . . 41
### Consult Supervisors and Appropriate Legal Counsel . . . 42

## Conclusion . . . . . . . . . . . . . . . . . . . . . . . . . . . . . . . 43

## Endnotes . . . . . . . . . . . . . . . . . . . . . . . . . . . . . . . . 45

## Appendix A: Individual State Summaries of Mandatory Reporting Requirements 2011 . . . . . . 61

# Introduction

Social workers may find themselves torn between their commitment to their clients' interests and their responsibility to the larger society when faced with the possibility of reporting child abuse to authorities.[1] "Since the 1960's social workers throughout the United States have been required to disclose confidential information, sometimes against a client's wishes, to comply with mandatory reporting laws on child and elder abuse and neglect."[2] Social workers were initially concerned about the requirements' effects on their relationships with clients; however, "social workers now recognize the public's compelling interest in this social policy."[3]

For social workers, the reporting of child abuse represents far more than an ethical dilemma. Mandatory reporting laws not only require social workers to report suspected cases of child abuse and neglect, but also there can be varying levels of civil and criminal liability for failing to do so. For example, a social worker at a family services agency failed to report an incident of child abuse he witnessed during a counseling session to "preserve the therapeutic relationship."[4] The parent involved later killed his child, and the social worker was charged with a criminal offense for his failure to comply with the state's mandatory reporting law. The level of attention given to these issues by federal and state governments emphasizes the importance society places on the need for intervention on behalf of children victimized by abuse.

As captured in federally collected data for the reporting year 2010, an estimated 695,000 children were the victims of maltreatment.[5] Among these children, those in the age group of birth to one year were the most frequently victimized. Girls were more frequently harmed—51.2 percent versus 48.5 percent for boys—and neglect was the most reported violation at more than 75 percent of the reports.[6] However, more than 15 percent of the victims suffered physical abuse, and another 9 percent suffered sexual abuse.[7] Tragically, during the reporting period, approximately 1,560 children died due to neglect and abuse,[8] and most of these children—nearly 80 percent—were younger than four years old. Of the fatalities, boys had a higher rate.[9] Because of mandatory reporting requirements, three-fifths of all reports of child abuse came from professionals—including medical personnel; law enforcement; educators; lawyers; and social service workers, including professional social workers. "The three largest percentages of FY 2010 reports were from . . . educational personnel (16.4%), law enforcement and legal personnel (16.7%), and social services staff (11.5%)."[10]

This law note discusses the legal issues social workers confront when dealing with child abuse and neglect situations. First, this note provides a brief history of the federal legislation that established mandated federal standards for CPS and the reporting of suspected child abuse. Second, this note surveys state statutes and case law, providing an overview of the current state of mandatory reporting laws (Appendix A summarizes each state's reporting requirements). Third, it identifies the various ethical considerations social workers face in meeting their reporting obligations. Fourth, it discusses emerging issues related to child abuse reporting that may be complex and require further analysis. Finally, it provides practical steps for reporting child abuse.

Please note that federal and state laws and court interpretations continue to develop and change. As a result, legal advice must be tailored to the specific facts and circumstances of a particular case. This note is designed to provide you with a general overview of many of the issues presented in cases of child abuse and neglect. However, nothing reported herein should be used as a substitute for the advice of competent counsel. If you have any questions or concerns applicable to a specific situation, please seek legal advice.

# Federal Legislation—The Child Abuse Prevention and Treatment Act of 1974 (CAPTA)

Congress enacted the Child Abuse Prevention and Treatment Act in 1974.[11] CAPTA's goals were to provide a uniform, national standard for combating child abuse and neglect, provide funds for state child abuse programs, and promote awareness of the issues surrounding child abuse and neglect. Although all states had passed child abuse reporting statutes, CAPTA provided minimum national standards states must meet to qualify for federal funding.[12] CAPTA was reauthorized and expanded in 2003 by the Keeping Children and Families Safe Act of 2003.[13]

Prior to CAPTA, there was little public recognition of the impact of child abuse and neglect nationwide. Published in 1962, C. Henry Kempe's groundbreaking research on child abuse is often credited as the major impetus behind the creation of these national goals.[14] Through a study of 302 severely injured children from 71 hospitals, Kempe introduced a new medical term, "battered child syndrome," into the public arena.[15] This empirical study helped legitimize concerns about the pervasiveness of child abuse in the United States and widely publicized the issue for the first time nationally.[16]

Further research found that the professional community did not report the numerous child abuse cases it saw on a daily basis. Rather than alerting authorities, professionals would often ignore, rationalize, or even fail to recognize the signs of child abuse.[17] Although aware of the state reporting laws, some professionals believed that if they were mistaken they would be subject to criminal and civil lawsuits. These perceived risks resulted in the nonreporting of many child abuse cases.[18] Many professionals were simply not trained or equipped to file a report. It was soon recognized that federal legislation was necessary to help broaden awareness and allow for individuals to report suspected child abuse without fear of civil or criminal liability.[19]

With CAPTA, Congress provided for the allocation of funds to the states for the identification, treatment, and prevention of child abuse.[20] CAPTA was designed with three goals in mind: (1) standardizing the process of reporting child abuse, (2) enhancing the states' ability for further inquiry or treatment of child abuse, and

(3) focusing public awareness on the immunity provided for reporting suspected child abuse.[21]

## CAPTA Requirements

CAPTA sets minimum requirements for states to provide a structure for reporting, investigating, and protecting abused children. In return for following these guidelines, states receive federal funds to support their enforcement programs.[22] States are mandated to provide:

- a program that has provisions or procedures for the reporting of known and suspected instances of child abuse and neglect;
- procedures for the immediate screening, safety assessment, and prompt investigation of such reports;
- procedures for immediate steps to be taken to ensure and protect the safety of the abused or neglected child;
- provisions for immunity from prosecution under state and local laws and regulations for individuals making good faith reports of suspected or known instances of child abuse or neglect; and
- methods to preserve the confidentiality of all records to protect the rights of the child and of the child's parents or guardians.

## Minimum Acceptable Definitions

CAPTA provides minimum, standard definitions for the terms "child," "child abuse and neglect," "sexual abuse," and "withholding of medically indicated treatment."

Section 5106(g) defines a child as a person who has not attained the age of 18, or, in the case of sexual abuse, the age specified by the child protection law of the state in which the child resides.[23]

Child abuse and neglect is, at a minimum, any recent act or failure to act on the part of a parent or caretaker, which results in death, serious physical or emotional harm, sexual abuse or exploitation, or an act or failure to act that presents an imminent risk of serious harm.[24]

Sexual abuse is defined broadly to include "the employment, use, persuasion, inducement, enticement, or coercion of any child to engage in, or assist any other person to engage in, any sexually explicit conduct or simulation of such conduct for the purpose of producing a visual depiction of such conduct." The definition also includes "rape, and in cases of caretaker or inter-familial relationships, statutory rape, molestation, prostitution, or other forms of sexual exploitation of children, or incest with children."[25]

CAPTA defines the withholding of medically indicated treatment as "the failure to respond to the infant's life-threatening conditions by providing treatment (including appropriate nutrition, hydration, and medication) which, in the treating physician's or physicians' reasonable medical judgment, will be most likely to be effective in ameliorating or correcting all such conditions." The definition explicitly exempts failure to provide treatment when the infant is "chronically and irreversibly comatose," the treatment merely prolongs dying and would not heal the infants' conditions, or the treatment itself would be inhumane under the circumstances.[26]

# State Statutes

Since the enactment of the federal guidelines, all 50 states have modified, amended, or enacted statutes mandating the reporting of child abuse.[27] All states provide a definition of child abuse that incorporates some or all of the following elements: nonaccidental physical injury, neglect, sexual molestation, and emotional abuse.[28] The states' reporting statutes also establish a process for reporting suspected abuse, a list of mandatory reporters, and guidelines for what must be reported.[29] It is important to recognize that each state reporting law has its own definitions and requirements, and it is critical that social workers be familiar with the laws of their state. Specifically, there are three key questions that must be asked: (1) Who is required to report; (2) What is required to be reported; and (3) When is reporting required?[30]

## Definitions

In general, the maltreatment of any child under the age of 18 must be reported.[31] Unlike CAPTA, state statutes tend to separately define neglect and abuse.[32] Child neglect includes "withholding necessary food, clothing, shelter, and educational opportunities, or other forms of inadequate care and supervision that might lead to endangering the child's wellbeing."[33] "Failure to thrive" denotes a subcategory of neglect that encompasses the withholding of love, socialization, and proper stimulation from the child.[34] Child abuse includes physical, sexual, and mental maltreatment of a child.[35] It is often difficult to distinguish between neglect and abuse under the state definitions. An abusive situation (physical maltreatment) can lead to a neglectful situation. A child suffering from a pattern of physical or sexual abuse may not be eating or sleeping properly, not attending school, and experiencing emotional problems.[36]

Legal definitions of abuse and neglect serve three functions: (1) identifying criminal acts, (2) determining child dependency, and (3) identifying cases that warrant reporting. As noted, these legal definitions often overlap. This leads to significant difficulties in determining what warrants a report, especially where the definitions vary considerably.[37] Some forms of maltreatment are not defined in state statutes, such as poverty-related neglect, emotional maltreatment, educational neglect, and medical neglect.[38] Thus, knowing the statutory definitions may not always be a useful way of determining what must be reported. Skillful clinical evaluation and continued therapeutic intervention with the child and family may be critical in monitoring relevant details that could form the basis for a credible report that meets the legal criteria as the case develops.

Finally, these legal definitions focus on two aspects of abuse: (1) the behavior of the abusive individual, and (2) the effects of the abuse or the harm suffered by the child.[39] The five primary terms that states invariably provide definitions for are child, physical abuse, sexual abuse, neglect, and emotional maltreatment.[40] Each of these terms is examined below.

## Child

Although it is a seemingly easy task, the most fundamental definition that must be addressed is the definition of "child." As noted above, CAPTA defines a child as someone who has yet to attain the age of 18.[41] Most state statutes only provide a fixed end point defining when a person is no longer legally a child. Statutes have not identified when a person first becomes a "child" for purposes of child abuse and neglect statutes. Most state courts that have examined this issue have determined that under the rules of statutory construction and interpretation, "child" and "person" do not include a viable fetus.[42]

South Carolina is the only state to recognize a "viable fetus" as a "child."[43] In *Whitner v. State*, a pregnant mother admitted to ingesting crack cocaine during the third trimester of her pregnancy and pled guilty to a neglect charge under South Carolina Code Ann. § 20–7–50. South Carolina Code defined neglect as "having the legal custody of any child ... [and] neglect[ing] to provide ... proper care and attention. ..."[44] On appeal, the court was presented with the question of whether a viable fetus is a "person" for purposes of the neglect statute. Although recognizing other states' courts presented with the issue had found to the contrary, the South Carolina court held "it would be absurd to recognize the viable fetus as a person for purposes of homicide laws and wrongful death statutes, but not for purposes of statutes proscribing child abuse."[45]

Questions regarding how "child" is defined are also found when dealing with emancipated minors. "Emancipated minor" is generally defined as "a person under eighteen years of age who is totally self-supporting."[46] This is a legal determination made by a court following a hearing or other judicial process. A few states make specific mention of emancipated minors.[47] The majority of states, however, make no distinction between a "child" and an "emancipated minor" under the reporting statutes. Thus, any child, even an emancipated one, would fall within the statutory definition in many states.

## Physical Abuse

Physical abuse is generally defined as some injury that has not occurred by accident. Physical abuse definitions focus on the harm or injury to the child, not to the specific acts of an abuser. Texas, for example, defines abuse as an "injury that results in substantial harm to the child, or the genuine threat of substantial harm from physical injury to the child, including an injury that is at variance with the history or explanation given and excluding an accident or reasonable discipline by a parent, guardian, or managing or possessory conservator that does not expose the child to a substantial risk of harm."[48]

Because of the way physical abuse is often defined, social workers must use independent judgment to determine whether the harm the child has suffered or is likely to suffer is "substantial" and whether the harm is "accidental."[49] Given the ambiguities in the various definitions, it may be impossible to determine whether an injury falls within the statutory guidelines for mandatory reporting without a period of further observation and the accumulation of additional facts.[50] "Thus, although on the surface physical abuse would appear to be readily detectable and, therefore, reportable, perhaps more than any other type of abuse, suspicions of physical abuse are complicated by numerous definition problems."[51]

There are dozens of possible signs of physical abuse. Some include unexplained physical injuries such as burns, bites, bruises, broken bones, or black eyes, fading bruises or other noticeable marks after absences from school, fear of parents or adults, shrinking away from adults when they approach, and reports of injuries of the child from a parent or other child caregiver.[52] In determining "accidental" injuries, warning signs include inconsistent stories of the accident, a delay in seeking care, unrealistic expectations of the child by the caregiver, frequent hospital visits and use of multiple hospitals, and claims of a triggering behavior of the child that causes the abuse.[53]

## Sexual Abuse

Sexual abuse, unlike physical abuse, has few outward signs of harm. Legal definitions tend to focus on the conditions and circumstances where sexual abuse often occurs. For example, Mississippi defines sexual abuse as "obscene or pornographic photographing, filming or depiction of children for commercial purposes, or the rape, molestation, incest, prostitution or other such forms of sexual exploitation of children under circumstances which indicate that the child's health or welfare is harmed or threatened."[54] Some states have adopted the broad definition provided by CAPTA that includes any sexually explicit conduct or simulation.[55] Others have not defined sexual abuse at all.[56]

Possible signs of child sexual abuse include difficulty walking and sitting, adult-level sexual knowledge, pregnancy, and contraction of a sexually transmitted disease. A child may be withdrawn or depressed, have bloody underclothing, and may report that genitalia have been played with or touched.[57] Behavioral changes include fear or dislike of certain people, sleep disturbances, headaches, acting out in school, withdrawal from family, poor hygiene, discipline problems, eating disorders, self-destructive activities, hostility and aggression, suicide attempts,[58] drawings that show sexual activity, bedwetting, and performing or attempting to perform sexual acts with other children.[59]

## Neglect

Neglect is generally defined as a "failure" to provide some kind of needed care for the child. Whereas abuse requires a harmful action by the caregiver, neglect focuses on inaction or omission by the caregiver.[60] Arkansas has one of the more extensive definitions for neglect. Under the Arkansas definition, neglect includes "failure or refusal to prevent abuse, ... to provide the necessary food, clothing, shelter, and education required by law, or medical treatment, ... to take reasonable action to protect ... from abandonment, abuse, sexual abuse, sexual exploitation, neglect or parental unfitness ... or to assume responsibility for the care and custody ... or participate in a plan to assume such responsibility."[61]

Possible signs of neglect include frequent absences from school, begging or stealing food from classmates, lacking adequate medical and dental care, wearing inadequate clothing during cold weather, abusing drugs and alcohol, and the child reporting that no one is at home to care for him or her.[62]

## Emotional Maltreatment

Emotional maltreatment definitions tend to look to the signs of injury to the child, rather than the circumstances surrounding the maltreatment. Much like physical abuse, emotional maltreatment definitions focus on an examination of the child in determining whether maltreatment has occurred.[63] Also referred to as mental cruelty or emotional neglect, emotional maltreatment occurs when nonphysical abuse resulting in physical or psychological illness is inflicted on a child.[64] Minnesota has listed emotional harm as a form of neglect, that results from a "pattern of behavior which contributes to impaired emotional functioning of the child which may be demonstrated by a substantial and observable effect in the child's behavior, emotional response, or cognition that is not within the normal range for the child's age and stage of development, with due regard to the child's culture."[65]

Possible signs of emotional maltreatment include extreme swings in mood and behavior, inappropriate adult behavior or inappropriate infantile behavior, severe delays in physical or emotional development, suicide attempts, and showing no attachment to adults at an early age.[66]

## Corporal Punishment

Corporal punishment of children has a long history[67] and is disturbingly prevalent in U.S. society.[68] It generally refers to noninjurious hitting for the purpose of modifying a child's behavior.[69] Corporal punishment may currently legally occur in the home, and in some states corporal punishment is permitted in schools. At home, parents and guardians in all 50 states have a right to discipline their children, including the use of physical discipline.[70] State child abuse statutes have created exceptions for *reasonable* physical punishment inflicted on children by their parents,[71] therefore distinguishing between lawful and unlawful forms of corporal punishment.[72] The task of differentiating between reasonable physical punishment and child abuse requires social workers to exercise professional discretion based on their training, experience, and knowledge of the definitions of abuse and neglect in the state in which they are practicing. Although mandated reporters may face consequences for false reporting of child abuse and for the failure to report it, states also provide immunity from civil and criminal liability for reporting in "good faith," so that mandated reporters have statutory support for reporting in close cases.[73]

Corporal punishment is prohibited in most juvenile detention centers and in foster care settings. However, 21 states do allow corporal punishment to be used in schools. It "usually takes the form of paddling (also called 'swats,' 'pops,' or 'licks')."[74] According to the U.S. Department of Education, 7.5 percent of Mississippi public school students were paddled in the 2006–07 school year, the highest percentage in the nation.[75] Federal law also permits the use of reasonable corporal punishment in schools.[76] Some states have criminalized excessive corporal punishment and placed limitations on the amount of hits a student may receive.[77] Mandatory reporters of child abuse, such as teachers and social workers, may need to distinguish between reasonable corporal punishment and child abuse in the course of deciding whether a report to child protection officials is required, depending on the explanation given as to the cause of a child's injuries or distress.

Many of the criticisms of corporal punishment have been focused around its disproportionate usage for minority students,[78] and its general negative effects on children's psyche. "Researchers found that corporal punishment is not better than other discipline methods at promoting long-term compliance or moral internalization (that is, the child's internalizing positive moral values), and in fact may be worse by decreasing these positive behaviors."[79] Studies have also found that frequent use of corporal punishment may cause aggressive behavior, antisocial behavior, and even lead to mental health problems, like depression or anxiety in children.[80] Many academic and professional organizations, including the National Association of Social Workers (NASW), oppose the use of corporal punishment in schools.[81]

## Problems of Ambiguity in State Definitions

Even a well-informed social worker may have difficulty determining which specific situations require reporting given the ambiguities inherent in the many state definitions. In some cases, careful review of the controlling state statute is not sufficient to avoid confusion. Because states recognize the importance of the statutory definitions in determining reporting requirements, most state statutes provide broad definitions. These broad definitions ensure that social workers err on the side of reporting, thus giving the state a greater chance of a successful intervention in potentially abusive situations. However, with an increase in the number of substantiated reports, states also run the risk of receiving many more unsubstantiated reports.[82] Although narrower definitions may have less ambiguity, they come at the risk of underreporting.[83] Reporting criteria of state statutes, consequently, span a continuum of broad definitions of abuse and low standards of certainty that abuse has occurred.

It is also important to know what behaviors are not legally defined as child abuse. Certain situations or circumstances that alone may not be child abuse or neglect include fights between children,[84] the use of reasonable force to stop a threat of physical injury by law enforcement (such as to obtain possession of weapons or other dangerous objects within the control of a child),[85] recognized spiritual or religious practices,[86] reasonable parental discipline,[87] sexual activity between minors,[88] and environmental factors that are beyond the control of the parent such as inadequate housing, furnishings, income, clothing and medical care.[89]

# Mandated Reporters

Certain individuals, on the basis of their profession, skills, or likely contact with abused children, are required to report any suspected cases of child abuse. These individuals are called "mandated reporters."[90] When states first introduced mandatory reporting statutes, many targeted medical professionals only.[91] Physicians opposed being given the burden of being the primary detectors of child maltreatment and argued mandatory reporting violated doctor-patient confidentiality and the ethical duty owed to patients.[92] These arguments were unsuccessful, and as states continued to pass mandatory reporting statutes, the medical profession sought, in the alternative, to add other professions to the list. As a consequence, the number of professions legally required to report suspected child abuse has continually expanded.[93] Today, a majority of states provide a list of professionals who are considered mandatory reporters.

There are approximately 40 different professions specifically named in reporting laws.[94] Generally, these lists are categorized and identify professions involved in contact with children on a regular basis.[95] For example, California lists 28 professional categories including health practitioners, child care custodians,[96] child protective agency employees, firefighters, animal control officers, humane safety officers, commercial film and photographic print processors, clergy members, and law enforcement officials.[97] Illinois has a lengthy list of over 55 professions and professional categories that are mandated to report suspected child abuse.[98] Each state has its own list of mandatory reporters, and some states include professions not commonly found in other states. For example, Colorado includes veterinarians,[99] Nevada includes school librarians,[100] and in Wisconsin dieticians are required to report.[101]

Some states have opted to include all individuals, regardless of profession, as mandatory reporters.[102] Some states have chosen, in lieu of an "all persons" requirement, to modify the language to be slightly more restrictive. Alabama, for example, restricts the requirement to "any person called on to render aid to a child."[103] Washington state's statute specifies "adults who reside" with the child are mandatory reporters, in addition to the list of professional reporters.[104] Regardless of the "all people" mandates in some jurisdictions, every state includes social workers on their mandatory reporter list.[105] Some states are more specific in this regard. Kansas, for example, specifies "licensed social worker[s],"[106] whereas Oregon requires "licensed clinical social workers"[107] to report.

It is important to recognize that anyone *may* report suspected child abuse, whether or not defined as a mandatory reporter. One does not have to be a "social worker" or any other "professional" to report suspected child abuse.[108]

The varying statutes defining who is mandated to report can have meaningful consequences when applied to real fact situations. For example, in *H.B. by and through Clark v. Whittmore*,[109] a Minnesota trailer park manager was found not to have the duty to report child abuse, despite having been notified by the abuser of the abuser's previous convictions for child abuse and knowing that children were spending excessive amounts of time with the abuser.[110] Minnesota is not an "all persons" state and only health care, social services, education, child care, and law enforcement professionals are required to report.[111] Similarly, in *M.H. v. Barber*,[112] another Minnesota case, a nonprofit private corporation that performed foster care licensing and evaluation was found to have no duty to a friend of a foster care child who was sexually abused in the foster care home.[113]

# Reporting and Reporting Procedures

A social worker does not need specific or substantial evidence that child neglect or abuse has occurred, nor does the reporter need to witness the neglect or abuse. State statutes generally require a reasonable cause to believe or to suspect that abuse has occurred.[114] This standard provides flexibility and allows social workers to use their best judgment in determining whether to report.[115] The primary question a social worker must ask when applying the given circumstances to the state definitions and the signs of child abuse and neglect is: would "a reasonable person ... have reasonable cause to believe that a child has been abused?"[116] Given the significance of this kind of decision, one author on child abuse suggests that "if in doubt, resolve the doubt in favor of the child, and report."[117]

The two most common standards in the state statutes are "reasonable grounds (or cause) to believe"[118] and "reasonable cause to suspect."[119] Although a careful weighing of the differences between a belief and a suspicion would seem to find "believe"[120] to be a higher degree of certainty than "suspect,"[121] for the purposes of mandatory reporting statutes, an individual should consider them equal. For example, Kentucky uses "believe" in its statute, stating "when [social workers] know or have reasonable cause to believe that a child is dependent, neglected, or abused."[122] Mississippi uses "suspect" in the statute, stating "when [social workers] have reasonable cause to suspect that a child is an abused or neglected child."[123] The two statutes have similar standards, and, other than the "belief" and "suspect" language, there is no substantial difference between them.[124]

If a social worker has made the determination that a reasonable belief or suspicion of child abuse exists, the social worker must act by reporting pertinent information to the state designated agency.[125] In general, this could include local law enforcement,[126] the state department of children or health and social services,[127] a central intake or registry,[128] CPS,[129] a designated child welfare agency,[130] or, as is one option for Tennessee, the "judge having juvenile jurisdiction."[131] As a general matter, most states rely on both local law enforcement and state executive departments of health or public welfare. All states provide either a 24-hour telephone hotline or a combination of alternatives to ensure suspected child abuse can be reported at any time.[132]

## Jurisdiction

Where to report is sometimes as difficult a question to answer as whether to report. Some states have specific guidelines regarding where reports should be made, especially if the child resides in a different locality than the one where the discovery of abuse was made.[133] In general, there are three primary options states may choose to resolve this issue. Suspected abuse should be reported either to (1) the local authorities where the child resides, (2) the local authorities where the reporter resides, or (3) the local authorities where the suspected abuse is taking place.[134] For example, Tennessee requires reports be made "where the child resides."[135] Ohio requires reports "in the county in which the child resides or in which the abuse or neglect is occurring or has occurred."[136] Oregon, however, requires reports be made "where the person making the report is located at the time of the contact."[137]

## Acceptable Time Frame for Reporting

Most state statutes use the phrase "shall immediately report" when describing the time frame in which a social worker is expected to make an initial report, whether in person or over the telephone.[138] Alternatives to the "immediately" requirement include "within 12 hours,"[139] "within 24 hours,"[140] "promptly,"[141] "as soon as possible,"[142] "immediately, but in no event later than 24 hours,"[143] "immediately, no more than forty eight hours,"[144] and "first opportunity, no longer than 48 hours."[145] A handful of states do not require reporting within a specific time period.[146]

## Content of Reports

Having made contact with the appropriate authorities, the social worker has statutory obligations to provide specific information to the extent known. This generally includes the name and age of the minor, the address of the minor, the name of the person responsible for the child's care (a parent, custodian, or guardian), and the extent and nature of the suspected abuse.[147] Social workers and other professionals must provide the authorities with his or her name and address.[148] Discretionary reporters, however, are generally not required to identify themselves.[149] The reporter's name and address should be kept confidential by the authorities.[150]

Some states require a subsequent written report from a social worker.[151] Other states make a written report necessary only if requested by the state agency.[152] A written report should detail the same information given in the oral report and any other evidence or pertinent information that may be helpful in investigating the suspected abuse or neglect.[153] The Massachusetts reporting statute states:

A report filed under this section shall contain: (i) the names and addresses of the child and the child's parents or other person responsible for the child's care, if known; (ii) the child's age; (iii) the child's sex; (iv) the nature and extent of the child's injuries, abuse, maltreatment or neglect, including any evidence of prior injuries, abuse, maltreatment or neglect; (v) the circumstances under which the person required to report first became aware of the child's injuries, abuse, maltreatment or neglect; (vi) whatever action, if any, was taken to treat, shelter or otherwise assist the child; (vii) the name of the person or persons making the report; (viii) any other information that the person reporting believes might be helpful in establishing the cause of the injuries; (ix) the identity of the person or persons responsible for the neglect or injuries; and (x) other information required by the department.[154]

## When Reporting Responsibility Ends

In most social work settings, the agency will have a process for reporting suspected child abuse. When child abuse is suspected, social workers must be concerned not only with when to report, but also where their responsibility to report ends. In *Commonwealth v. Allen*,[155] a teacher and a school counselor followed school policy and reported suspected child abuse to the school's principal. The principal, however, did not forward the information to the authorities.[156] The Kentucky Supreme Court held the teacher and counselor were not relieved of their statutory obligation under the Kentucky reporting statute, despite following school protocol. The court reasoned "there is no guarantee that a supervisor will follow through with the duty and relay the report to governmental authorities."[157]

A number of states and the District of Columbia have codified this nondelegable reporting duty. The duty requires that a social worker is obligated to ensure a report is made to the authorities even if that individual has followed an internal reporting protocol.[158] Simply notifying a superior of suspected child abuse or neglect may not be sufficient to comply with the statute and allow the social worker to avoid liability. Other states relieve the social worker of the responsibility after following a formal policy, such as reporting abuse to a supervisor.[159] A majority of states have not codified where the social worker's duty ends. It is recognized in some states, however, that once a report has been made, a social worker is not required to file additional reports.[160]

## Privileged Communication Exception

In keeping with public policy that the protection of children generally supersedes the confidentiality of communications,[161] states have been willing to cast aside the common law and statutory doctrines of privileged communications[162] in relation to mandated child abuse reporting. In all states with statutory recognition of the social worker–client relationship, mandatory reporting requirements supersede or abrogate the statute.[163] Case law in states having litigated this issue confirms the paramount importance of reporting child abuse and neglect over client confidentiality.[164]

Although social workers must provide necessary information regarding suspected child abuse, they do not necessarily have to provide more. The duty to report abuse, by itself, does not diminish the privilege of confidentiality between a client and professional in any other area (assuming the state recognizes the social worker–client privilege).[165] If called to testify, however, professionals may have an ethical dilemma regarding what they may or may not disclose, particularly treatment notes.

Courts have clarified that social workers are obligated to notify clients of the "child abuse" exception to confidentiality. In *State v. Shirah*,[166] the client believed he had an absolute privilege of communication with his social worker. In the course of his communications, he divulged he was abusing his two adopted daughters. The social worker later testified against the client in a criminal prosecution.[167] On appeal, the client (perpetrator) argued that he was not informed of the child abuse exception to privileged communications. Although recognizing the statutory privilege of communication between social worker and client, the court held that, on the basis of the record, the client should have been aware of the exception.[168] The court further concluded "social workers and other mandatory reporters should advise patients of the statutory duty to report instances of child abuse, the non-confidential nature of communications, and the potential use of the communications in a criminal prosecution."[169] This is also considered sound clinical practice and is an ethical obligation articulated in the NASW *Code of Ethics*.[170]

# Immunity

Before the passage of CAPTA, the fear of being sued for libel, slander, defamation, invasion of privacy, or breach of confidentiality was a primary deterrent hindering the reporting of suspected child abuse, although this fear was generally unfounded.[171] CAPTA requires that all states have "provisions for immunity from prosecution under State and local laws and regulations for individuals making good faith reports."[172] Accordingly, all states have granted criminal and civil immunity to reporters acting in good faith.[173] This, however, does not prevent the filing of a lawsuit claiming damages for wrongful reporting. Statutory immunity only makes it difficult for such a suit to succeed. Any complaint failing to establish sufficient allegations of bad faith reporting may be generally dismissed before trial.[174]

## Good Faith Requirement

Almost all states require "good faith"[175] reporting—that is, a factual showing of the reasons the report was made.[176] When the social worker evidences "good faith," the burden shifts to the accuser to show the absence of good faith, or in other words, bad faith. The absence of good faith is shown by evidence the reporter acted maliciously, because of prejudice or personal bias, recklessly or with gross negligence in their decision to report.[177]

A representative survey of case law shows that it is difficult for the accuser to meet this evidentiary standard. In *Parker v. Venture, Inc.*,[178] a Louisiana case, the court found "without knowledge that the information was false or with reckless disregard whether it was false, [it] must find that the report was made in good faith."[179] In *D.L.C. v. Walsh*,[180] a Missouri case, the negligent misdiagnosis and reporting of suspected child sexual abuse by a physician did not prevent "good faith" immunity.[181] The court in *L.A.R. v. Ludwig*,[182] an Arizona case, recognized the mandate to report based on "reasonable grounds" to believe abuse took place is a low standard, and consequently, the accuser must prove the reporter's malice to prevail in court.[183] The court also noted the immunity statute is applicable only to the reporting of child abuse—any other claims of negligence against the reporter are not subject to immunity.[184]

Some states do not specifically require good faith, but instead provide immunity unless the report was made with "malice,"[185] "in bad faith,"[186] or "grossly negligent."[187]

# Good Faith Presumption

Instead of requiring a reporter to affirmatively prove that they have acted in good faith, several states have created a presumption of good faith in reporting suspected child abuse.[188] The applicable Wyoming statute reads:

> Any person, official, institution, or agency participating in good faith in any act required or permitted by [the reporting laws] is immune from any civil or criminal liability that might otherwise result by reason of the action. For the purpose of any civil or criminal proceeding, the good faith of any person, official, or institution participating in any act permitted or required by [the reporting laws] shall be presumed.[189]

In jurisdictions with a good faith presumption, accusers must prove the child abuse report was not made in good faith to prevail in their claim. In *Heinrich v. Conemaugh Valley Memorial Hospital*,[190] a Pennsylvania case, the court concluded the plaintiff could not overcome the statutory presumption on the facts alleged. Accordingly, the court dismissed the suit on summary judgment and the case went no further.[191]

# Absolute Immunity

Finally, three states, California, New Jersey, and Ohio,[192] have provided absolute immunity[193] to mandatory reporters. Ohio's statute provides absolute immunity for reporting suspected child abuse only and "good faith" immunity for other connected actions.[194] California's statute is broader, providing immunity to social workers even if the report is negligently, knowingly,[195] or intentionally false.[196]

For example, in *Walters v. Enrichment Center of Wishing Well, Inc.*,[197] an Ohio case, the plaintiffs alleged day care center employees reported them for suspected child abuse in retaliation for filing a police report against the center. The court held the reporters were "immune from any claims arising out of the filing of the report … regardless of whether the report was made in good faith."[198] In New Jersey, in *Rubinstein v. Baron*,[199] the court stated "This court can only conclude that the [reporter] has an absolute privilege. Thus, the fact that the [reporter] may have acted with malice is irrelevant."[200] In *Stecks v. Young*,[201] a California case, the court concluded absolute immunity would be granted, regardless of reasonable suspicion, irrelevant statements, or untimely written reports. In this case, the licensed counselor who reported the suspected abuse allegedly acted solely on the accusations of an allegedly schizophrenic sufferer of multiple personality disorder. The client had no personal knowledge any child was being abused, but the counselor made a report to the authorities.[202] This was done without communicating with the parents or the children identified as being participants in satanic rituals and human sacrifices. Here, even the court "express[ed] [its] concern that factually this case presses the outer limits of immunity."[203]

# Failure to Report

In most jurisdictions, failure to report on the part of a social worker may result in criminal liability. To a lesser degree, some states have made social workers open to civil liability based on a failure to report child abuse.

## Criminal Liability

In nearly all jurisdictions, a social worker may be held criminally liable for failure to report child abuse. In general, the state must be able to prove beyond a reasonable doubt subjectively that the reporter "knowingly" or "willfully" failed to report.[204] A few states require proof beyond a reasonable doubt using an objective standard.[205] As a misdemeanor, penalties range in monetary fines up to $1,000 and imprisonment of up to one year. In proving that a reporter had "reason to believe" or "reasonable cause to believe" as is required in most statutes, prosecutors can use evidence that is both circumstantial (suspicious, "accidental" injuries; signs of deprivation; parental indifference; and so forth), or direct (eyewitness to abuse, child's description, observing parental inability to care for child).[206] Given the difficulty of proving whether one had a reasonable belief or reasonable cause to believe beyond a reasonable doubt, most cases are either dismissed before trial, end in acquittal at trial, or are reversed on appeal.[207] Regardless of the success rate in prosecuting nonreporters, social workers should view the possibility of their being prosecuted for a failure to report seriously.[208]

One important item to note is that failing to report does not equal acting as an accomplice to abuse.[209] Absent an affirmative act by the nonreporter, such as covering up evidence of abuse, reporters generally cannot be considered accomplices. Knowing a crime has occurred and failing to report it is not considered affirmative assistance in committing the act of child abuse.[210] Although criminal liability would not attach, all social workers should keep in mind that their failure to report abuse may potentially assist an abuser, and that this assistance is potentially damaging to more than just a single child, given the statistical likelihood of abuse or molestation of more than one child.[211]

## Civil Liability

There are a number of different ways a social worker who fails to report can be held accountable under civil law.[212] In some states, statutes provide for civil liability. In others, common law doctrines such as negligence per se and general tort theories of liability may apply. Finally, plaintiffs may also be successful pursuing a claim of professional malpractice against the reporter. Each of these issues will be discussed below.

# Statutory Civil Liability

In addition to criminal penalties, failure to report may leave a social worker open to monetary damages through private action on behalf of the child. This civil liability is explicitly recognized by statute in a number of states.[213] In Michigan, the state statute that authorizes civil action for a failure to report reads:

> A person who is required by this act to report an instance of suspected child abuse or neglect and who fails to do so is civilly liable for the damages proximately caused by the failure. A person who is required by this act to report an instance of suspected child abuse or neglect and who knowingly fails to do so is guilty of a misdemeanor punishable by imprisonment for not more than 93 days or a fine of not more than $500.00, or both.[214]

These states limit liability to social workers who fail to report to situations when they "knowingly" or "willfully" fail to report.[215] "The 'knowing' or 'willful' standard for liability is narrower than the ordinary tort standard of 'negligence.' It is usually adopted to avoid penalizing would-be reporters for honest mistakes in interpreting the difficult and ambiguous facts surrounding most cases of child maltreatment."[216] These standards are similar to those found in the criminal statutes, however a civil penalty generally requires a far less substantial burden of proof than a criminal charge does. A prosecutor seeking to hold a reporter criminally liable must prove a "knowing" or "willful" failure to report beyond a reasonable doubt. In a civil case, however, the standard is generally a preponderance of the evidence.[217] Thus, in states where civil liability is statutorily authorized, a private plaintiff may have greater success in moving forward a civil claim than the state would on the same charges brought in a criminal case.

For the vast majority of states without explicit statutory language authorizing private actions against reporters, the question of whether a private action against a mandated reporter can be brought remains ambiguous. To determine whether a private right of action exists, courts will generally look to the legislative history of the act. "In the absence of specific statutory language, generally, the test whether an individual right of action exists for violation of a statute is whether the legislature intended to give such a right."[218] Three state courts that have considered this issue have determined that no private cause of action exists absent an express grant of authority by the legislature.[219] In *Valtakis v. Putnam*,[220] a child victim of sexual abuse sued officials who were responsible for the supervision of a probationer who abused him. Although the court recognized the officials' failure to report was a crime, it determined the officials could not be held financially responsible under the same statute.[221] Similarly, a Kansas court held in *Kansas State Bank & Trust Co. v. Specialized Transportation Services, Inc.*,[222] that "there is no express indication of legislative intent to impose any liability for failure to report" within the statute, and therefore, no private cause of action.[223]

# Negligence Per Se

Negligence per se is a common law doctrine that allows for an automatic finding of negligence if the act committed was a violation of a state statute.[224] In the mandatory reporting context, at least one state allows plaintiffs to go forward with a civil suit solely on the basis of the state child abuse statute, having found that the statute itself can be used to determine whether a social worker has been negligent in his or her duties.[225] To find negligence per se, a court must determine that (1) a reporter violated a statutory duty by failing to report, (2) the child suffered subsequent injuries, (3) the failure to report was the proximate cause of those injuries, (4) the statute was designed to protect against those types of injuries, and (5) the child was within the class of people protected by the statute.[226] To be held liable under a negligence per se standard, the individual who fails to report must be a mandatory reporter.

In *Alejo v. City of Alhambra*, the California Court of Appeals held a claim of negligence per se was appropriate against a police officer who failed to report suspected child abuse.[227] Although commentators agree that this is a logical appropriate view of state reporting statutes,[228] at least one state has declined to follow California's lead.[229]

# General Common Law Tort Theory

Other states have found that their statutes do not provide for civil liability or negligence per se. Consequently, an individual must rely on common law tort theories such as malpractice. In general, for plaintiffs to prevail on a tort-based cause of action, they must show that the defendant had a legal duty to the injured person, the defendant breached this duty, the failure to perform the duty is the proximate cause of the injury, and that the court is capable of providing a remedy for the injury.[230]

In civil actions using failure to report as the cause of action, plaintiffs may use the violation of a state mandatory reporting statute as evidence of "negligence" on the part of the person who failed to report. However, absent some doctrine like negligence per se, the use of the state mandatory reporting statute is much less effective. It will simply be one piece of evidence, among many, that will be weighed by the jury to determine whether the reporter breached a duty to the plaintiff. [231]

Under the common law, determining whether a duty exists is exceedingly difficult. General tort common law has established the precedent that an individual does not generally have a duty to affirmatively come to the aid of another, even in an emergency.[232]

## Professional Malpractice

Professional malpractice is a tort-based theory that alters the common law elements of a tort by raising the standard of care. Under general common law tort theories, the standard of care is an objective one: that of "the reasonable person in like circumstances." When a plaintiff, however, can establish that the nonreporter is a professional, the standard of care rises to the level of a professional in similar circumstances.[233] Recognizing that professionals, by virtue of their training and expertise, should be held to a higher standard of care, the common law holds a professional to the "reasonable professional in his or her profession in similar circumstances" standard, rather than the "reasonable person" standard. In defending against a malpractice charge, professional standards are usually established through the use of professional standards and codes. When the defendant is a social worker, a plaintiff would use the NASW *Code of Ethics* and other practice standards to establish what the reasonable social work professional should have done.[234] Although there is little case law holding a "social worker" to a "professional standard" in the specific area of reporting child abuse, it has occurred,[235] and there is no reason to believe that the standard is not applicable to social workers. The NASW *Standards for Clinical Social Work in Social Work Practice* states:

> Social workers should be familiar with national, state, and local exceptions to confidentiality, such as mandates to report when the client is a danger to self or others and for reporting child or elder abuse and neglect. The clinical social worker shall advise the client of confidentiality limitations and requirements at the beginning of treatment. Professional judgment in the use of confidential information shall be based on best practice, as well as legal, and ethical considerations.[236]

## Intentional False Reporting

To prevent intentional false reporting of child abuse, a majority of states[237] have enacted statutes imposing criminal sanctions against individuals who "willfully," "knowingly," "intentionally," or "maliciously" make false reports.[238] Most of these states classify false reporting as a misdemeanor.[239] Three states, Florida, Tennessee, and Texas, classify it as a felony.[240] Michigan takes a novel approach and classifies the offense based on what the falsely accused abuser would have received. If the falsely accused abuser's crime would have constituted a misdemeanor, then the false report is classified as a misdemeanor; likewise, if the crime would have constituted a felony, the false report is classified as such.[241]

The states provide penalties, usually including jail time and monetary fines, like most misdemeanor provisions.[242] Idaho and Minnesota demand the offender pay civil actual damages.[243] As an example of false reporting, the Colorado statute provides the following:

> No person, including [a mandatory reporter], shall knowingly make a false report of abuse or neglect to a county department or local law enforcement agency. Any person who violates [this provision] commits a Class 3 misdemeanor and shall be punished [as provided by law]; and shall be liable for damages proximately caused thereby.[244]

Intentionally making a false report subjects the reporter to civil liability for the injury caused to the individual the report was made against and the local government for the wasted resources a false complaint expends. States that do not have specific false reporting statutes for child abuse have general criminal statutes that can be relied on. For example, Illinois states, "any person who knowingly transmits a false report to the Department of Children and Family Services commits the offense of disorderly conduct under the law."[245]

# Ethical Considerations

"Social workers often have access to sensitive information about intimate aspects of clients' lives, including information about personal relationships, domestic violence, substance abuse, sexual trauma and behavior, criminal activity, and mental illness ... [to] assess clients' circumstances thoroughly ... and implement appropriate intervention."[246] Although social workers should obtain only essential information as part of their professional functions, any private information obtained by the social worker must be protected to the greatest extent possible.[247] NASW has codified these principles in the *Code of Ethics*:

1. Rule 1.07(a) — Social workers should respect clients' right to privacy. Social workers should not solicit private information from clients unless it is essential to providing services or conducting social work evaluation or research. Once private information is shared, standards of confidentiality apply.[248]
2. Rule 1.07(b) — Social workers may disclose confidential information when appropriate with valid consent from a client or a person legally authorized to consent on behalf of a client.[249]

One of the most common exceptions to confidentiality is the disclosing of private information pertaining to suspected abuse or neglect of a child. The NASW *Code of Ethics* explicitly provides for this exception to client confidentiality.[250]

> Rule 1.01 — Commitment to Clients — Social workers' primary responsibility is to promote the well-being of clients. In general, clients' interests are primary. However, social workers' responsibility to the larger society or specific legal obligations may on limited occasions supersede the loyalty owed clients, and clients should be so advised. (Examples include when a social worker is required by law to report that a client has abused a child or has threatened to harm self or others.)[251]

Furthermore, "the general expectation that social workers will keep information confidential does not apply when disclosure is necessary to prevent serious, foreseeable, and imminent harm to a client or other identifiable person."[252]

When a social worker (or other mandatory reporter of child abuse) must determine whether a specific set of facts constitutes child abuse or neglect, there are two general scenarios that may result. In the first scenario, the social worker reports the suspected child abuse to the appropriate authorities.[253] The authorities, in turn, make a determination of whether to accept the report and either investigate or close the case. In 2007, only 24.1 percent of suspected child abuse and neglect reports were substantiated, and 61.3 percent of the reports were unsubstantiated.[254] The *Fourth National Incidence Study on Child Abuse and Neglect* concluded that during the 2005–06 time period, 68 percent of the children in their study were identified as abused or neglected yet never investigated.[255] Through investigation, alleged child abuse may be substantiated or not. Victims of child abuse slip through the cracks when real abuse cases are never investigated or closed on the basis of a false, unsubstantiated determination.[256] In such cases, the social worker has complied with the legal mandate of reporting, but has arguably hampered the therapeutic process by breaching confidentiality[257] and relying on the protective system to provide the necessary intervention.

In the second scenario, if the social worker decides for documentable reasons, not to report the suspected abuse, the child may continue to be a victim of abuse.[258] The social worker may also take on the responsibility of protecting the child or may attempt to provide services to the abuser. If it is later determined that there is no abuse, the child and family would be saved from a probing, accusatory investigation.[259] Yet even in that scenario, the social worker may be at risk of criminal and civil liability for not abiding by reporting laws.

The social worker must decide whether the protective services agency should be relied on to deal with the abuse or neglect. Unfortunately, statistics concerning the performance of protective services agencies are troubling.[260] In 2009, the National Center on Child Abuse and Neglect reported that 38.1 percent of child abuse allegations received by CPS were "screened out," meaning the allegations of abuse did not meet the agency criteria and would not be investigated.[261] Out of the allegations investigated, about a quarter of the reports found one or more victim of maltreatment, while "two-thirds of reports found all allegations to be unsubstantiated or intentionally false."[262] Studies empirically demonstrate that there is a lack of reporting "real" child abuse while there is an over-reporting of "false" or mistaken child abuse.[263]

Many, therefore, without disputing the ethical duty to report, disagree with the process by which the reporting statutes are implemented.[264] It has been argued that the current system diverts resources to the investigation of unfounded reports and away from serious cases. Recommendations to improve this system include clarifying the abuse reporting laws by drafting narrower definitions,[265] increasing public and professional education,[266] screening reports and rejecting those that do not fall within definitions,[267] giving feedback to people who report,[268] and providing a proper support structure for reporters.[269] Some have also suggested that the mandatory reporting statutes be repealed.[270]

# Issues Involving CPS Workers

In addition to their role as mandatory reporters, social workers often find themselves in the position of receiving reports of child abuse and neglect, primarily in CPS or other child welfare positions. In addition to the duties imposed on social workers by the mandatory reporting statutes, many of these same statutes impose duties on the social workers who receive reports and are required to act on them.

State reporting laws generally require CPS to notify law enforcement or local prosecutors immediately or as soon as is practicable on receipt of a report from a mandatory reporter.[271] However, it is important to note that although social workers are generally covered by immunity for reporting suspected child abuse, the actions they may take in a CPS capacity to remedy the child abuse may leave them open to liability.

The U.S. Supreme Court in 2011 declined to address whether search warrants are required to conduct child abuse investigations in a school. In *Camreta v. Greene*, an appeal from the U.S. Court of Appeals for the Ninth Circuit,[272] the Supreme Court held that the appeal was moot because the child had moved out of the Ninth Circuit's jurisdiction and was nearly an adult. In a very narrow ruling, the Supreme Court reversed the Ninth Circuit's decision requiring a warrant or parental consent before a child welfare official may interview a child at school to investigate whether the child was a victim of suspected sexual abuse.[273]

The case arose in Oregon in 2003 when an experienced caseworker, Mr. Camreta, was assigned to investigate a child's safety after a report of possible sexual abuse by her father. Camreta, accompanied by a deputy sheriff, interviewed the child in a private room at her school without obtaining her parent's consent. On the basis of the information Camreta gathered during the interview, he believed the child had been abused. The father was later indicted for sexual abuse of his daughter, and ordered not to have any contact with her, although the criminal charges were ultimately dismissed.[274]

The child's mother filed an action for damages in federal court against Camreta and the Deputy Sherriff. She alleged they violated her daughter's Fourth Amendment rights by interviewing her without parental consent or a warrant, and that they violated the mother's Fourteenth Amendment rights by preventing her from being with her daughter during a medical examination.[275] The District Court granted summary judgment to the Oregon officials. The mother appealed and the U.S. Court of Appeals for the Ninth Circuit agreed with the mother on the warrant issue but upheld the District Court's conclusion that the Oregon officials were entitled to the protection of qualified immunity from damages because there was no established requirement for a warrant. The Ninth Circuit did view the child's interview by a case worker and sheriff to be an interrogation and unreasonable seizure in violation of her Fourth Amendment rights.[276] The court also found that parents have a familial right to be with their children during such examinations, and if a valid reason exists to exclude them from the exam room, they have a right to be close by in the waiting room.[277]

Although the U.S. Court of Appeals for the Ninth Circuit decision to uphold the summary judgment favored the Oregon officials, they sought review of the Ninth Circuit's ruling that their conduct violated the Fourth Amendment. On appeal, the U.S. Supreme Court was asked to address the following questions:

- Does the Fourth Amendment require a warrant, a court order, parental consent, or exigent circumstances before law enforcement and child welfare officials may conduct a temporary seizure and interview at a public school of a child whom they reasonably suspect was being sexually abused by her father?
- Is the Ninth Circuit's constitutional ruling reviewable, notwithstanding that it ruled in petitioner's [Camreta] favor on qualified immunity grounds?[278]

In an opinion written by Justice Kagan, a majority of the U.S. Supreme Court determined that certain cases can be reviewed, regardless of a favorable ruling below on qualified immunity, but that this particular case was moot because the child was no longer subject to any potential harm by these government officials, because she had moved to Florida and was nearing her 18th birthday.[279] In addition, the Supreme Court vacated the U.S. Court of Appeals for the Ninth Circuit's decision that had required a warrant to interview a child at school to investigate possible abuse or neglect.[280] The Supreme Court's ruling has a narrow application that may remove the immediate threat of sanctions for CPS investigators who do not obtain a warrant in the Ninth Circuit, but it falls short of providing clear guidance to child protection officials across the nation.[281] "The tenor of the [Supreme] Court's questions during oral argument" suggests that "it 'would not necessarily agree with the 9th Circuit on the merits,'" but it remains unresolved.[282]

NASW filed an *amicus curiae* ("friend of the court") brief in support of DHS's authority to conduct joint interviews at children's schools and provided the U.S. Supreme Court with social science and policy information supporting the practice of multidisciplinary interview protocols.[283] The NASW *Camreta* brief also highlighted the central purpose of CAPTA as a civil scheme to protect children supported by the federal law's legislative history. Recognizing the trauma of child abuse and the conduct of investigations, states are continuing to develop investigative approaches that afford child victims the sensitivity and protection that they require. The *Camreta* brief referenced the unfortunate reality that in homes in which sexual abuse occurs, both parents may have strong incentives to deter children from disclosing embarrassing family secrets.

In an earlier California-based case in which the removal of two children from a home because of suspected child abuse was challenged, the social workers in that case were held civilly liable for doing so without first obtaining a search warrant.[284] Despite the argument that the social worker was following county protocol in removing without a warrant, the U.S. Court of Appeals for the Ninth Circuit held that the law was clearly established that removal of children in a nonemergency child abuse context required a search warrant.[285]

The investigation of suspected child abuse can present a myriad of challenges, both practical and legal, many of which are beyond the scope of this law note.[286] It is important that social workers acting in a CPS capacity know and understand the child abuse reporting laws and regulations in their applicable states and consult with appropriate legal counsel to effectively investigate allegations while respecting the legal rights of children and families.

# Emerging Issues

A number of issues that can confound social workers in practice involve mandatory reporting such as the use of adult memories of childhood abuse, cross-jurisdictional reporting and implications of technology-based activity, including "sexting." These issues often present "grey" areas without bright-line legal guidance. Consultation with CPS, state social worker licensing boards, supervisors, professional associations, or attorneys may be necessary to develop an appropriate response. These issues are discussed in detail below.

## Adult Survivors of Abuse and Adult Recovered Memory

The revelation of child abuse and neglect after the child has reached the age of majority raises a number of issues with mandatory reporting laws. As they are currently structured, the mandatory reporting laws are not clear as to whether a social worker who learns of past child abuse from a victim who is now an adult is required to report. Although the public policy goals of the mandatory reporting program generally focus on protecting children from abuse and neglect, rather than prosecuting abusers, it is unclear whether a social worker would be held liable for failure to report abuse reported by an adult that occurred during the adult's childhood. Given the media attention of the last few years on issues of child abuse by members of the clergy,[287] cases of child abuse reported by adults long after the abuse has ended have become more common.

Although case law in this area is sparse, an Attorney General Opinion in Maryland expresses the view that a report is required, even if the abuser is deceased.[288] However, Ohio and Texas have determined that a report is not mandatory if the victim is no longer a child.[289] In one reported case on point, clergy members in Pennsylvania were not required to report child sexual abuse of an individual who was abused as a minor but did not reveal the abuse to the defendants until after reaching the age of majority.[290] However, if it is determined that a third party is in harm's way (for example, when an adult daughter discloses that she now remembers being abused by her father and there are currently children in the father's home), it is the duty of the social worker to report and take the necessary steps to prevent possible harm.[291] For example, the state of Washington provides that,

> The reporting requirement does not apply to the discovery of abuse or neglect that occurred during childhood if it is discovered after the child has become an adult. However, if there is reasonable cause to believe other children, dependent adults, or developmentally

disabled persons are or may be at risk of abuse or neglect by the accused, the reporting requirements shall apply.[292]

Social workers confronted with this situation should review the laws of the jurisdiction and may also contact their local child welfare agency or other official recipient of child abuse reports to determine if a report is necessary. Of course, adults with a history as child abuse victims may voluntarily choose to report the abuse to authorities, regardless of therapists' obligations, and this is sometimes a clinically significant act of client self-empowerment.

Distinctions may be drawn between cases in which an adult who is a psychotherapy client for the first time recalls sexually abusive activity that occurred in their childhood (that is, "recovered memory")[293] and instances in which a psychotherapy client has always retained a memory of childhood abuse, but discloses it for the first time to the therapist (that is, "delayed disclosure"). The concept of recovered memory has received increased attention over the past two decades[294] and should be treated differently from delayed reporting.

When recollections of abuse result in civil litigation against the alleged abuser, seeking compensation for the abuse the adult had to withstand as a child and the aftereffects that have been carried into adulthood, the victim–survivor's therapist may become a target of litigation by the alleged abuser, accusing the therapist of creating memories of events that did not occur.[295] The courts have split on whether to accept recovered memory claims and allow the presentation of evidence on this concept because of its scientific unreliability.[296] Regardless, whenever a social worker is providing services to an adult survivor of child abuse, the matter of reporting or not reporting the allegations may have serious professional consequences that require thorough review.

## Cross-Jurisdictional Cases

In general, the state mandatory reporting laws focus on in-state reporting of abuse by social workers who reside in the same state as the perpetrator and victim. However, in some situations—especially in cases involving telepractice or e-therapy—the social worker may not always be in the same jurisdiction as the client. Each state has its own procedures governing the reporting of child abuse and neglect, but generally the first step requires phone contact with a designated state agency. Determining which state agency is appropriate—the state agency of the state in which the social worker is practicing, or the agency of the state in which the child is located or resides or in which the abuse occurred—may be difficult. This difficulty can be exacerbated in the case of children with multiple residences, as may occur in custody situations where the divorced parents live in different states and the child spends portions of time with each custodial parent.

In situations in which there is a question regarding jurisdiction, social workers should contact their local CPS or other governmental agency for advice on where to report cross-jurisdictional abuse.

# Child Pornography

Social workers may find themselves counseling adults who admit during treatment to possession and viewing of child pornography. Because of the potential for serious criminal penalties to be imposed against violators of child pornography laws and the difficulties in establishing an effective therapeutic relationship with child abusers, it is important that social workers be aware of the legal requirements in their state for reporting child pornography activity.

The "possession, production, or distribution of child pornography" is a federal crime and convicted individuals must register as a sex offender in the jurisdictions where the person resides, was convicted, and is employed.[297] Furthermore, social workers engaged in professional activity on federal land or in a federal facility must comply with federal child abuse reporting requirements, and report any suspected child abuse.[298] The federal statute defines "child abuse" as the "physical or mental injury, sexual abuse or exploitation [defined as child pornography[299]], or negligent treatment of a child."[300]

Child pornography is defined under federal law as:

> any visual depiction, including any photograph, film, video, picture, or computer or computer-generated image or picture, whether made or produced by electronic, mechanical, or other means, of sexually explicit conduct, where (A) the production of such visual depiction involves the use of a minor engaging in sexually explicit conduct; (B) such visual depiction is a digital image, computer image, or computer-generated image that is, or is indistinguishable from, that of a minor engaging in sexually explicit conduct; or (C) such visual depiction has been created, adapted, or modified to appear that an identifiable minor is engaging in sexually explicit conduct.[301, 302]

Among state laws, the definition of child pornography varies. Some states have adopted the language of the federal statute,[303] whereas others have created their own definition and penalties.[304] However states must comply with the federal sex offender registration system, or forfeit 10 percent of the federal funding they would have otherwise received.[305] Additionally, some states have passed their own legislation mandating the registration of sex offenders, which may include people convicted for possessing and distributing child pornography.[306]

The rise of the Internet has also fueled a significant increase in the trafficking of child pornography produced by adults. Although the creation and dissemination of child pornography was relatively difficult just 20 years ago, today it is both inexpensive and easily transmitted.[307] At the same time, cracking down on child pornography has become a major focus of law enforcement at both the state and federal levels.

Three different scenarios involving child pornography may involve social workers and mandatory reporting statutes. The first scenario involves an individual viewing or having viewed child pornography. The second scenario involves an individual in possession of child pornography or engaged in its distribution to others. The third scenario involves the creation of child pornography by the individual.

Of these three scenarios, the most clearly reportable is the situation in which the individual is creating or has created child pornography. Creation of child pornography necessarily must involve direct contact with a child, and, thus, under most state law definitions of child sexual abuse or sexual exploitation, this type of behavior must be reported immediately.

The scenario involving viewing of child pornography created by a third party is problematic, given that most definitions of child sexual abuse do not include reviewing prohibited content, separate from some involvement with a specific child. However, as the American Prosecutors Research Institute notes, "the victimization of the children involved does not end when the pornographer's camera is put away … the pornography's continued existence causes the child victim continuing harm by haunting those children in future years."[308] Nevertheless, in the absence of knowledge that the viewer of child pornography has engaged in other suspicious conduct involving direct contact with minors, it may be difficult to pinpoint a reporting requirement.[309] The distinction between viewing child pornography and "possessing" it may be as fine as determining whether the content was intentionally downloaded to the user's computer or mobile phone.

The scenario involving distribution of child pornography clearly violates criminal laws, but there may be some ambiguity as to whether it falls within the scope of the child abuse reporting requirements.[310] Reviewing the statutory definitions of abuse in a social workers' state is an important element in determining how to handle this situation in clinical practice. Given the grave harm to victims of child pornography, the ethical and legal exceptions to social workers' confidentiality standards would generally be considered to permit the reporting of this activity to prevent serious, imminent, and foreseeable harm to children.[311] The question of whether such reporting is required in each case is a more complicated matter.

The complexities of this area of concern are growing because of the interstate and transnational trafficking of children for sexual exploitation, raising questions about conflicting laws and enforcement authority. Social workers are strongly urged to consult with their local CPS, child welfare agency, or police authorities if they have questions regarding the standards for reporting activity involving child pornography. Cases in which a social worker does not find a basis for mandated reporting may still involve completing a competent clinical assessment of the client to make an appropriate referral for specialized treatment of sexual disorders. Social workers who are inexperienced with treating sex offenders or sexual disorders should identify services within the community or in specialized treatment programs to assure that potential predators or abusers receive the necessary intervention to address their conditions and protect the public. Prevention of child sexual abuse and exploitation can be a successful outcome of early treatment by a skilled clinician or continued treatment may serve to uncover reportable misconduct that is then addressed through the legal and child protection systems. In no case is it recommended that a clinician rely solely on treatment as an alternative to reporting conduct that falls within the mandatory child abuse reporting laws. The dilemmas created by situations such as child pornography highlight the importance for social workers to review with clients at the initiation of treatment the limits of confidentiality, including the obligation to report activity that may be considered harmful to children.

# "Sexting"

Technological advances have revolutionized personal communication, especially the proliferation of mobile phone technology. In 2009, 88.1 percent of the population of the United States had mobile phones.[312] According to a recent study, 58 percent of 12 year olds own a mobile phone, while 83 percent of 17 year olds do.[313] Nearly 75 percent of the population has Internet access.[314] Although the dangers of online predators and sexual abuse of children through the Internet are well-known,[315] technological advances in mobile phone and digital camera technology, especially in the hands of children, present a new area of concern for social workers.

One of these new areas is referred to as "sexting," in which individuals send "sexually suggestive nude or nearly nude images or videos of themselves to someone else via text messaging."[316] Given the availability of mobile phone cameras with e-mail and text capability, sexting is an area in which the potential for child sexual abuse is expanding. A 2009 Pew Internet and American Life Project study found 4 percent of mobile-phone-owning children ages 12 to 17 admit sending sexually suggestive nude or nearly nude images of themselves to someone else via text messaging.[317] Fifteen percent admit receiving a sexually suggestive image of someone they know.[318] Seventeen year olds lead the numbers, with 8 percent admitting having sent an image, while 30 percent have received one.[319]

The states have yet to develop a common approach to handling sexting. Generally, mandatory reporting statutes tend to define child sexual abuse broadly, and the transmission of explicit photographs between adults and children is likely to be reportable.[320] This is consistent with the purpose of child protection laws: to protect children from predators and pedophiles.

In some jurisdictions, law enforcement has threatened children who voluntarily sent photos to friends with prosecution for child pornography.[321] This is especially troubling, given that in many instances, the victim is often the perpetrator. In *Miller v. Mitchell*,[322] a teenage girl who was threatened with prosecution for felony child sexual abuse if she did not attend an educational program directed at sexting offenders successfully challenged the prosecutor's actions in federal court. The appeals court upheld the trial court's ruling (on a preliminary motion) that the plaintiff can show that requiring her to attend the education program "would violate her First Amendment freedom against compelled speech."[323]

Legal scholars have opined that prosecutors and courts should differentiate between consensual sexual conduct between teens, which is generally not criminalized or subject to mandatory reporting,[324] and nonvolitional sexting, which occurs when sexually graphic photos are sent electronically to third parties without the consent of the individual depicted in the photo.

> Aside from the fact that [consensual] sexting does not constitute child abuse or exploitation, prosecuting teens for sexting under child pornography laws fails to protect children because the punishment under these laws is much more harmful than the underlying conduct. For example, a conviction under a child pornography statute may require a teen to register as a sex offender. The stigma that this punishment carries will follow the teen throughout much, if not all, of his or her life. While a provocative photo of a teen *may* have negative effects on his or her future, for example if a college admissions staff discovers it on the Internet, being registered as a sex offender undoubtedly will negatively [a]ffect the teen's future [internal citations omitted].[325]

However, given the ease of distributing electronic images, it is difficult to determine the dividing line between consensual sexting and nonconsensual distribution of sexually explicit images of children. Thus, it is unclear whether a social worker who discovers that a child has engaged in this behavior would be required to report it under the mandatory reporting statutes. In at least one reported instance, a mandated reporter was charged with a misdemeanor for failing to report abuse after the individual (a school principal) confiscated a student's cell phone containing a sexually explicit picture.[326]

There is no doubt that the harms from nonvolitional sexting can be severe. A typical scenario involves a teen who sends a photo to a romantic partner and later becomes a victim of harassment, humiliation, and exploitation after the relationship ends and the photo is distributed to others without permission. A notable case is that of Jessica Logan, a student who eventually committed suicide as a direct result of the humiliation she experienced from severe and pervasive peer harassment after a nude photo of her was sent to classmates. Her parents brought civil suit against the students, now adults, who allegedly harassed her, against the school board for failing to protect her, and against law enforcement personnel.[327]

The states have begun to address sexting in legislation and they are using a variety of approaches, including attempting to define sexting, creating youth diversion programs, creating new misdemeanor crimes, or granting immunity to those who destroy a nude image when received or "report it to authorities within 48 hours."[328]

A valuable step for a social worker is to review the definitions of child abuse and child sexual abuse in the state child abuse laws (see Appendix A) to determine whether a particular sexting scenario presented by a client meets the definition for mandatory reporting. Where a decision regarding reporting obligations is unclear, it is best, at a minimum, to consult with the local child protection agency regarding legal requirements. Sound practice requires that the reasons for the consultation and the outcome be documented in the clinical notes.

# Practical Steps for the Social Worker

## Verify Reporting Duty with Local Authorities

As noted above, every state has specific legal requirements and rules for social workers. Thus, it is important for social workers to become familiar with the requirements of the state in which their practice is located.[329] A brief summary of each state's key reporting requirements is found in Appendix A. This law note introduces several of the major aspects of each state's enforcement scheme, but is neither intended to substitute for familiarity with the statutes in the social worker's state of licensure or practice, nor intended to substitute for the advice of counsel.

## Understand the Signs of Abuse

As previously mentioned, there are four major types of abuse: physical abuse, sexual abuse, neglect, and emotional maltreatment.[330] For a review of the signs of each, see the Definitions subsection under State Statutes, earlier in this note.

## Understand the Process of Investigation

Typically, CPS functions in any jurisdiction are underfunded and understaffed. Frustration can grow quickly when the social worker and the child authorities do not communicate.[331] It is important to understand how the agency that has jurisdiction functions when reporting abuse and neglect, if not before. The social worker should request a copy of the agency's procedures, reporting requirements, investigation standards, and goals.[332] On appropriate cases, the social worker may request to be updated on the status of the investigation. These cases would include those in which the child is the client or in which the social worker's relationship is based on the social worker's employment, such as a school, hospital, or daycare center.

## Document the Details

When social workers report suspected child abuse, accurate records should be kept of every action made by the social worker, from a written summary of the reported incident to documentation of the conversation with the authorities over the phone. A factually correct report to the authorities will make it easier for them to determine whether a report should be investigated.[333] It will also provide evidence that the social worker has properly fulfilled the statutory duty.

# Consult Supervisors and Appropriate Legal Counsel

Whenever there is any question regarding the duty to report a particular situation or incident, the best course of action is to consult with supervisors and legal counsel. Those who understand the local legal system are best at providing sound advice. When available, legal consultation is helpful in determining whether reporting standards have been met and what should be included in the content of the report. Legal counsel can also provide a social worker with the status of the law in the jurisdiction, any current legislation, and any recent court decisions. Consultation with a supervisor may also assist in determining the statutory responsibilities of reporting. A social worker who has knowledge or suspects abuse, however, ultimately has the professional duty to act on that information, regardless of the recommendations of a supervisor. Although this may create professional dilemmas in certain cases, the social worker should attempt to work out the situation to ensure that the professional and legal requirements of reporting are met.

# Conclusion

Although the mandatory reporting of child abuse can be a highly charged issue, it is nonetheless the law in every jurisdiction in the United States. Responding appropriately to the legal mandate sometimes requires consideration of multiple factors, but the primary purpose of protecting children is clear. Social workers must use their knowledge of state law and their professional skills to determine if it is reasonable to believe abuse might have occurred. As mandatory reporters, social workers may have to violate client confidentiality to meet their legal obligations. Failing to report child abuse can result in criminal and/or civil liability.

Social workers in child welfare are also in the position to receive and evaluate reports of child abuse. Social workers working in CPS obtain such reports and have a legal obligation to respond to them. These social workers are faced with the additional challenges of investigating abuse in accordance with the legal standards established for the conduct of such investigations, which are not always clear. Much like reporting abuse, the investigation of suspected child abuse can present numerous professional challenges. It is important that social workers acting in a CPS capacity, or as mandatory reporters, understand applicable state child abuse reporting laws, and their obligations under those laws.

This note also provides references to other materials to allow social workers to continue their study of the issues found in each area. New issues are emerging in this field and have to be addressed every day by practicing social workers. These issues may present grey areas that require discussion with CPS, state social work boards, supervisors and experts in the field, or attorneys to properly address these matters.

Child abuse continues to be a major societal concern in the United States and the social worker's duty to report remains an essential part in the investigation and enforcement scheme adopted by state governments designed to save children from abuse and neglect. Knowledge of the social worker's obligations under applicable state law is necessary for responsible, competent practice.

# Endnotes

1. Frederik Reamer, Ethical Standards in Social Work 24 (2nd Ed. 2006); *see also* Seth C. Kalichman, Mandated Reporting of Suspected Child Abuse, Ethics, Law & Policy 52 (1993).
2. Frederik Reamer, Ethical Standards In Social Work 24 (2nd Ed. 2006).
3. *Id.*
4. *Id.* at 119.
5. U.S. Dept. of Health & Human Servs., Admin. for Children & Families, Admin. on Children, Youth and Families, Children's Bureau, *Child Maltreatment 2010*, 22–24 (2011), *available at* http://www.acf.hhs.gov/programs/cb/stats_research/index.htm#can.
6. *Id.*
7. *Id.*
8. *Id.* at 58–59.
9. U.S. Dept. of Health & Human Servs., Admin. for Children & Families, Admin. on Children, Youth and Families, Children's Bureau, *Child Maltreatment 2010*, 24–26 (2010), *available at* http://www.acf.hhs.gov/programs/cb/stats_research/index.htm#can.
10. *Id.*
11. 42 U.S.C. § 5106g.
12. *See generally* Nat'l Ass'n of Soc. Workers, Encyclopedia of Social Work 236 (Terry Mizrahi and Larry E. Davis eds., 20th ed. 2008) (discussing the history of child abuse reporting requirements).
13. P.L. 108-36.
14. Thomas Hafemeister, *Castles Made of Sand? Rediscovering Child Abuse and Society's Response*, 36 Ohio N.U. L. Rev. 819, 838 (2010).
15. C. Henry Kempe et al., *The Battered Child Syndrome*, 181 JAMA 17, 17–24 (1962) (stating "Battered-child syndrome is a term used to characterize a clinical condition in young children who have received serious physical abuse, generally from a parent or foster parent.").
16. Barbara Daly, *Willful Child Abuse and the State Reporting Statutes*, 23 Miami U. L. Rev. 283, 284–85 (1969); *See generally* Thomas Hafemeister, *Castles Made of Sand? Rediscovering Child Abuse and Society's Response*, 36 Ohio N.U. L. Rev. 819 (2010); Barbara J. Nelson, Making an Issue of Child Abuse (1984) (reconstructing the history of how individuals became concerned about child abuse and mobilized institutions in response).
17. Daly, *supra* note 16, at 306.
18. *See* Kalichman, *supra* note 1, at 13.
19. *See* Hafemeister, *supra* note 14, at 860.
20. 42 U.S.C. § 5103(b)(1) (1994), *repealed by* Child Abuse Prevention and Treatment Act Amendments of 1996, Pub. L. No. 104-235, 110 Stat. 3063, 3066.
21. *See* H.R. REP. No. 93-685, at 2–4 (1973), *reprinted in* 1974 U.S.C.C.A.N. 2763, 2765–66 (deciding that the federal government should support mandated child abuse reporting to state agencies).
22. 42 U.S.C. §§ 5101–5106 (2006).
23. 42 U.S.C. § 5106g(1).
24. 42 U.S.C. § 5106g(2).
25. 42 U.S.C. § 5106g(4).
26. 42 U.S.C. § 5106g(6).

27. Curt Richardson, *Physical/Hospital Liability for Negligently Reporting Child Abuse*, 23 J. LEGAL MED. 131, 134 (2002).

28. SHIRLEY O'BRIEN, CHILD ABUSE, A CRYING SHAME 72 (1980).

29. *Id.* at 103–07.

30. *Id.* at 9.

31. DOUGLAS J. BESHAROV, THE VULNERABLE SOCIAL WORKER, LIABILITY FOR SERVING CHILDREN AND FAMILIES 24 (1985); *see also* Maryann Zavez, *The Ethical and Moral Considerations Presented by Lawyer/Social Worker in Interdisciplinary Collaborations*, 5 Whittier J. Child & Fam. Advoc. 191, 209 (Fall 2005).

32. *See* O'BRIEN, *supra* note 28, at 8.

33. *See, e.g.*, Arkansas, California, District of Columbia, Idaho, Illinois, Maryland, Mississippi, and Texas. *But see, e.g.*, Georgia and Hawaii whose definitions of child abuse include both physical abuse and neglect.

34. *See* O'BRIEN, *supra* note 28, at 8.

35. *Id., see also* 42 U.S.C. § 5106 (g).

36. *See* O'BRIEN, *supra* note 28, at 8.

37. *See* KALICHMAN, *supra* note 1, at 25.

38. *Id.*

39. *Id.* at 26; *see also* ENCYCLOPEDIA OF SOCIAL WORK *supra*, note 12.

40. VERNON R. WIEHE, WORKING WITH CHILD ABUSE AND NEGLECT 47–80 (1996); *see also* JOHN MEYERS, THE APSAC HANDBOOK ON CHILD MALTREATMENT (3rd Ed. 2010).

41. 42 U.S.C. § 5106g(1).

42. *See, e.g., Cochran v. Commonwealth of Kentucky*, 315 S.W. 3d 325 (Ky. 2010); *Commonwealth v. Welch*, 864 S.W.2d 280 (Ky. 1993); *Kilmon v. State*, 905 A.2d 306 (Md. 2006); *Sheriff v. Encoe*, 885 P.2d 596 (Nev. 1994); *State v. Gray*, 584 N.E.2d 710 (Ohio 1992); *Reinesto v. Super. Ct.*, 894 P.2d 733 (Ariz. Ct, App. 1995); *Reyes v. Super. Ct.*, 75 Cal. App. 3d 214, 141 (Cal. Ct. App. 1977); *State v. Gethers*, 585 So. 2d 1140 (Fla. Dist. Ct. App. 1991); *State v. Luster*, 419 S.E.2d 32 (Ga. Ct. App. 1992); *State v. Martinez*, 137 P.3d 1195 (N.M. Ct. App. 2006); *Collins v. State*, 890 S.W.2d 893 (Tex. App. 1994); *State v. Dunn*, 916 P.2d 952 (Wash. Ct. App. 1996); *State v. J.Z.*, 596 N.W.2d 490 (Wis. Ct. App. 1999). The courts are careful to note that their decisions are based on statutory construction and the interpretation of the statutes, rather than on public policy grounds.

43. *See State v. McKnight*, 352 S.C. 635 (S.C. 2003); *Whitner v. State*, 492 S.E.2d 777 (S.C. 1997), cert. denied, 523 U.S. 1145 (1998). *But see*, WIS. STAT. ANN. § 48.981(2) (West 2009) (a Wisconsin statute providing that "any person … having reason to suspect that an unborn child has been abused or … at substantial risk of abuse may report").

44. *Whitner*, 492 S.E.2d at 779.

45. *Id.* at 780. For a medical discussion concerning the maternal ingestion of substances during pregnancy that cause fetal abuse, *see* Sana Loue, *Legal and Epidemiological Aspects of Child Maltreatment*, 19 J. LEGAL MED. 471 (1998). Nonconsensual drug testing used to facilitate the arrest and prosecution of mothers testing positive for cocaine has been held unconstitutional under the 4th Amendment. *See Ferguson v. Charleston*, 532 U.S. 67 (2001).

46. BLACK'S LAW DICTIONARY (9th ed. 1999), *available in* WESTLAW (defining emancipation as "the act by which a parent … frees a child and gives the child the right to his or her own earnings. This act also frees the parent from all legal obligations of support. Emancipation may take place by agreement between the parent and child, by operation of law … or when the child gets legally married or enters the armed forces").

47. *See, e.g.*, FLA. STAT. § 39.01(12) (2009) (defining a "child" as "any unmarried person under the age of 18 years who has not been emancipated by order of the court").

48. TEX. FAM. CODE ANN. § 261.001 (2007).

49. *See* Cincinnati Children's Hospital, *Detecting Child Abuse*, http://www.cincinnatichildrens.org/svc/alpha/c/child-abuse/faq/detect.htm (last visited April 13, 2011); Kenneth Lafontaine, Ohio State Uni-

versity Fact Sheet, *Recognizing Child Abuse and Neglect,* http://ohioline.osu.edu/4h-fact/0024.html; Ohio Children's Protective Services, *Detecting Child Abuse and Neglect,* http://cps.clermontcountyohio.gov/IdentifyingAbuse.aspx#PhysicalAbuse.

50. A few states specify "serious" harm. *See, e.g.,* IND. CODE ANN. § 31-34-1-2 (West 2009);" 23 PA. CONS. STAT. ANN. § 6303 (West 2008). The use of "serious" gives the reporter even more discretion. Serious injuries may include skull fractures, broken bones, and other significant injuries while "minor injuries include cuts, bruise, and other contusions not judged to be serious. *See* KALICHMAN, *supra* note 1, at 27.

51. KALICHMAN, *supra* note 1, at 27.

52. *See* Helpguide.org, *Child Abuse and Neglect, Recognizing and Preventing Child Abuse,* http://helpguide.org/mental/child_abuse_physical_emotional_sexual_neglect.htm (last visited April 8, 2011).

53. *See* Cincinnati Children's Hospital, *Detecting Child Abuse,* http://www.cincinnatichildrens.org/svc/alpha/c/child-abuse/faq/detect.htm (last visited April 13, 2011); Kenneth Lafontaine, Ohio State University Fact Sheet, *Recognizing Child Abuse and Neglect,* http://ohioline.osu.edu/4h-fact/0024.html (last visited April 13, 2011); Ohio Children's Protective Services, *Detecting Child Abuse and Neglect,* http://cps.clermontcountyohio.gov/IdentifyingAbuse.aspx#PhysicalAbuse (last visited April 13, 2011).

54. MISS. CODE ANN. § 43-21-105 (West 2008).

55. *See. e.g.,* ALA. CODE § 26-14-1 (2009).

56. *See, e.g.,* District of Columbia (defining 'sexual exploitation,' not abuse), Idaho (including forms of sexual abuse in the definition of "abused"), New Jersey (including sexual abuse in the definition of "abuse" but not defining it), and South Carolina.

57. *See* Ohio Children's Protective Services, *supra* note 53.

58. CHILDREN'S BUREAU, ADMINISTRATION ON CHILDREN, YOUTH AND FAMILIES, UNITED STATES DEPARTMENT OF HEALTH AND HUMAN SERVICES, RECOGNIZING CHILD ABUSE AND NEGLECT: SIGNS AND SYMPTOMS 3-4 (2007).

59. AMERICAN ACADEMY OF PEDIATRICS, HEALTH CHILDREN, *Safety and Prevention: Sexual Abuse* (2010), http://www.healthychildren.org/English/safety-prevention/at-home/Pages/Sexual-Abuse.aspx.

60. *See* KALICHMAN, *supra* note 1, at 28.

61. ARK. CODE ANN. § 12-18-103 (West 2009).

62. CHILDREN'S BUREAU, *supra* note 58, at 3.

63. *See* KALICHMAN, *supra* note 1, at 28. This form of maltreatment generally occurs in conjunction with sexual or physical abuse, but can occur by itself without the other forms of abuse.

64. *See* Helpguide.org, *Child Abuse and Neglect, Recognizing and Preventing Child Abuse,* http://helpguide.org/mental/child_abuse_physical_emotional_sexual_neglect.htm.

65. M.S.A. § 626.556 (2010).

66. CHILDREN'S BUREAU, *supra* note 58, at 4.

67. Gershoff, *More Harm Than Good: A Summary of Scientific Research on the Intended and Unintended Effects of Corporal Punishment on Children,* 73 SPG Law & Contemp. Probs. 31, 32 (2010):

> For centuries in this country and in countries around the world, corporal punishment of children occurred in a context in which such punishment was also acceptable as a means of punishing adults for infractions, often in the form of public floggings. But courts throughout the United States are no longer allowed to sentence criminals to corporal punishment, short of capital punishment. In contrast, corporal punishment of children by parents remains legal and accepted; in most states parents continue to have a legal defense against assault if their intention in hitting their children was to discipline them.

68. *See* Gershoff, *More Harm Than Good: A Summary of Scientific Research on the Intended and Unintended Effects of Corporal Punishment on Children,* 73 SPG Law & Contemp. Probs. 31, 31-32 (2010): "Roughly fifty percent of the parents of toddlers and sixty-five to sixty-eight percent of the parents of preschooler in the United States use corporal punishment as a regular method of disciplining their children. By the time American children reach middle and high school, eighty-five percent have been physically punished by their parents."

69. *See* Gershoff, *More Harm Than Good: A Summary of Scientific Research on the Intended and Unintended Effects of Corporal Punishment on Children*, 73 SPG Law & Contemp. Probs. 31 (2010).

70. Menendez, *When to Punish the Punishers, The New Standard for Corporal Punishment*, 10 Loy. J. Pub. Int. Law. 217, 218–219 (Spring 2009); *see also* Fla. Sta. Ann. § 39.01(2)("Corporal discipline of a child by a parent or legal custodian for disciplinary purposes does not in itself constitute abuse when it does not result in harm to the child.").

71. *See* Arkansas Code Annotated §12-8-103.

72. *See* Illinois: 325 Ill. Comp. Stat. Ann. 5/3; Nevada: NRS 432B. 150; New Jersey: N.J. Stat. Ann. § 9:6–8.9; Rhode Island: R.I. Gen. Laws § 40–11-2; South Carolina: S.C. Code Ann. § 20–7-490; Washington D.C.: D.C. Code Ann. § 16–2301; West Virginia: W. Va. Code § 49-1-3; Wyoming: Wyo. Stat. Ann. § 14-3-202.

73. Davidson, *When is Parental Discipline Child Abuse? The Vagueness of Child Abuse Laws*, 34 U. Louisville J. Fam. L. 403, 414–415 (1996); *see also* Art Hinshaw, *Mediators as Mandatory Reporters of Child Abuse*, 34 Fla. St. U. L. Rev. 271, 287 (2007).

74. The American Civil Liberties Union, A Violent Education: Corporal Punishment of Children in US Public Schools, 3–6 (2008), http://www.aclu.org/pdfs/humanrights/aviolenteducation_report.pdf.

75. *Id.* at 3 ("According to the Office for Civil Rights at the US Department of Education, 223,190 students nationwide received corporal punishment at least once in the 2006–2007 school year, including 49,197 students in Texas alone, the largest number of any state.").

76. *Id.* at 7; *see also Ingraham v. Wright*, 430 U.S. 651 (1977).

77. The American Civil Liberties Union, A Violent Education: Corporal Punishment of Children in US Public Schools, 7 (2008), http://www.aclu.org/pdfs/humanrights/aviolenteducation_report.pdf ("the standard of excessiveness is hard for students to prove ... [and] these regulations have proved difficult if not impossible to enforce.").

78. The American Civil Liberties Union, A Violent Education: Corporal Punishment of Children in US Public Schools, 5 (2008), http://www.aclu.org/pdfs/humanrights/aviolenteducation_report.pdf:

> In the 2006–2007 school year, African-American students made up 17.1 percent of the nationwide student population, but 35.6 percent of those paddled. In the same year, in the 13 states with the highest rates of paddling, 1.4 times as many African-American students were paddled as might be expected given their percentage of the student population. Although girls of all races were paddled less than boys, African-American girls were nonetheless physically punished at more than twice the rate of their white counterparts in those 13 states during this period.

*See also* Sacks, *State Actors Beating Children: A Call for Judicial Relief*, 42 UC Davis L. Rev. 1165, 1175–1176 (April 2009) (section dedicated to "Racial Disparities in Administration of School Corporal Punishment").

79. Gershoff, *More Harm Than Good: A Summary of Scientific Research on the Intended and Unintended Effects of Corporal Punishment on Children*, 73 SPG Law & Contemp. Probs. 31, 38 (2010).

80. *Id.* at 38–39, 43–44.

81. Sacks, *State Actors Beating Children: A Call for Judicial Relief*, 42 UC Davis L. Rev. 1165, at FN 152 (April 2009) (list of organizations that oppose corporal punishment in schools: American Academy of Child and Adolescent Psychiatry, American Academy of Family Physicians, American Academy of Pediatrics, American Counseling Association, American Association of School Administrators, American Bar Association, American Civil Liberties Union, American Humane Association, American Humanist Association, American Medical Association, American Orthopsychiatric Association, American Psychiatric Association, American Psychological Association, American Public Health Association, American School Counselor Association, Association for Childhood Education International, Association of Junior Leagues, Council for Exceptional Children, Defense for Children International, Friends Committee on Legislation, International Society for the Study of Dissociation, National Association for State Departments of Education, National Association for the Advancement of Colored People, National Association for the Education of Young Children, National Association of Elementary School Principals, National Association of Pediatric Nurse Practitioners, National Association of School Nurses, National Association of School Psychologists, National Association of Social Workers, National Association for State Boards of Education, National Council of Teachers of English, National Education Association, National Foster Parents Association, National Indian

Education Association, National Mental Health Association, National Organization for Women, National Parent Teachers Association, National Women's Political Caucus, Prevent Child Abuse America, Society for Adolescent Medicine, Unitarian Universalist General Assembly, United Methodist Church General Assembly, and the U.S. Department of Defense: Office of Dependents Schools Overseas).

82. "Substantiated" or "indicated" is often defined as a finding that there is satisfactory, credible evidence not refuted, that abuse, neglect, or sexual abuse has occurred. "Unsubstantiated" or "unfounded" is often defined as an insufficient amount of evidence to support a finding of abuse. See, e.g., MD. CODE ANN. FAM. LAW § 5–701 (West 2009).

83. See KALICHMAN, supra note 1, at 26.

84. CAL. PENAL CODE § 11165.6 (West 2009).

85. Id.

86. See, e.g., CAL. PENAL CODE § 11165.2 (stating treatment by spiritual means, not receiving treatment because of religious beliefs, or informed and reasonable decision by parent after consulting with physician does not alone constitute neglect); COLO. REV. STAT. ANN. § 19–3–103 (West 2009) (stating recognized method of religious healing alone not neglect); CONN. GEN. STAT. ANN. § 17a-104 (West 2009) (stating treatment by an accredited Christian Science practitioner alone is not neglect); DEL. CODE ANN. tit. 16, § 913 (2009) (stating 'good faith' treatment by a recognized church or religion solely by spiritual means through prayer alone is not neglect); Most states have some form of "religious belief" exception.

87. See, e.g., COLO. REV. STAT. ANN. § 19–1–103; FLA. STAT. ANN. § 39.01 (2) (West 2009); IND. CODE ANN. § 31–34–1–15; MISS. CODE ANN. § 43–21–105; MO. ANN. STAT. § 210.110 (West 2009); OHIO REV. CODE ANN. § 2151.031 (West 2009).

88. See, e.g., GA. CODE ANN. § 19–7–5 (b)(3.1) (West 2009) (exempting consensual sexual acts between minors or minors and adults less than 5 years older).

89. See, e.g., 23 PA. CONS. STAT. ANN. § 6303.

90. This note will use the term "social worker" interchangeably with the term "mandated reporter" or "mandatory reporter."

91. See KALICHMAN, supra note 1, at 23.

92. See id. at 24.

93. See generally Katharyn Christian, Putting Legal Doctrines to the Test: The Inclusion of Attorneys as Mandatory Reporters of Child Abuse, 32 J. Legal Prof. 215 (Spring 2008).

94. See KALICHMAN, supra note 1, at 24.

95. BECCA COWAN JOHNSON, FOR THEIR SAKE, RECOGNIZING, RESPONDING TO AND REPORTING CHILD ABUSE 54, (1992).

96. See People v. Hodges, 13 Cal.Rptr.2d 412 (Cal. App. Dep't Super. Ct. 1992) (finding that a pastor and an assistant pastor, acting as president and principal of a church school, were child care custodians under the statute and required to report child abuse). It is important to note, as Hodges demonstrates, that there can be diverse definitions of the professions included within mandatory reporting statutes.

97. CAL. PENAL CODE § 11165 (listing multiple professions within many of the professional categories, e.g. 14 specific medical professions within the health care worker definition).

98. 325 ILL. COMP. STAT. ANN. 5/4 (West 2009).

99. COLO. REV. STAT. ANN. § 19–3–304 (2010).

100. NEV. REV. STAT. ANN. § 432B.220 (2008).

101. WIS. STAT. ANN. § 48.981 (West 2009).

102. See, e.g., Delaware, Florida, Idaho, Indiana, Kentucky, Maryland, Mississippi, Nebraska, New Hampshire, New Jersey, New Mexico, North Carolina, Oklahoma, Rhode Island, Tennessee, Texas, Utah, and Wyoming.

103. ALA. CODE § 26–14–3 (2003).

104. WASH. REV. CODE ANN. § 26.44.030 (West 2009).

105. *See* Hafemeister, *supra* note 14, at 851.
106. Kan. Stat. Ann. § 38–2223 (2008).
107. Or. Rev. Stat. Ann. § 419B.005 (West 2009).
108. *See* O'Brien, *supra* note 28, at 104.
109. 552 N.W.2d 705 (Minn. 1996).
110. *See id.* at 707 (noting that when the children approached the manager for help, the manager only encouraged them to speak to their parents. After three more weeks of abuse, the children did inform their parents).
111. M.S.A. § 626.556.
112. *M.H. v. Barber*, No. C6–99–16, 1999 WL 343806, at *4, (Minn. Ct. App. June 1, 1999).
113. *Id.*
114. *See, e.g.*, Ala. Code § 26–14–3 (requiring a report "when the child is known or suspected to be a victim of child abuse or neglect"); Alaska Stat. § 47.17.020 (requiring a report when a mandatory report "[has] reasonable cause to suspect that a child has suffered harm as a result of child abuse or neglect").
115. *See* O'Brien, *supra* note 28, at 106; *see also F.A. by P.A. v. W.J.F.*, 656 A.2d 43, 44 (N.J. 1995) (holding that a neighbor's observation of children playing in the street, mother hysterically yelling at children, and child's broken leg created reasonable cause to suspect child abuse).
116. *F.A. by P.A v. W.J.F.*, 656 A.2d 43, 47(N.J. Super. Ct. App. Div. 1995) (The purposes behind mandatory reporting statutes include: (1) "Prevention of child abuse, (2) protection of children from abuse, and (3) preservation of family life when consistent with protection of children from abuse." *State v. Kitzman*, 920 P.2d 134, 139 (Or. 1996)(noting that "[T]he intent of the legislature was to protect children, not alleged perpetrators of child abuse, from potentially harmful investigatory techniques.")
117. O'Brien, *supra* note 28, at 106.
118. *See, e.g.*, Arizona, Georgia, Hawaii, Idaho, Illinois, Indiana, Iowa, Kentucky, Louisiana, Maryland, Massachusetts, Minnesota, Nebraska, Nevada, New Jersey, Oklahoma, Oregon, South Carolina, Texas, Utah, Vermont, Washington, and Wyoming.
119. *See, e.g.*, Alabama, Alaska, Arkansas, California, Colorado, Connecticut, Delaware, District of Columbia, Florida, Kansas, Maine, Michigan, Mississippi, Missouri, Montana, New Hampshire, New Mexico (suspicion), New York, North Carolina, North Dakota, Ohio, Pennsylvania, Rhode Island, South Dakota, Tennessee (indicate), Virginia, West Virginia, and Wisconsin.
120. Webster's New World Dictionary (4th College ed. 2004) (defining belief as "[t]o take as true, real; to have confidence in a statement or promise.").
121. *Id.* (defining suspect as "[t]o think it probable or likely; guess; surmise; suppose.").
122. Ky. Rev. Stat. Ann. § 620.030 (West 2009).
123. Miss. Code Ann. § 43–21–353.
124. One author makes a distinction between reasonable suspicions of abuse and "reason to believe or suspect," identifying that reasonable suspicion denotes an objective standard (as discussed above) and "reason to believe or suspect" denotes a more subjective standard. This latter terminology gives the social worker more discretion in deciding whether to report, making it much more difficult to enforce penalties for failure to report. *See* Kalichman, *supra* note 1, at 30. Thirteen states use this latter terminology. *See* Hawaii, Idaho, Indiana, Kansas, Maryland, Minnesota, New Hampshire, Oklahoma, Utah, and Virginia (using "reason to believe/ suspect") and Louisiana, North Carolina, and Texas (using "cause to believe/ suspect"). *But see*, Nevada, which uses both of these distinctions, "reason to believe" and "reasonable cause to believe."
125. *See* O'Brien, *supra* note 28, at 105–06.
126. *See, e.g.*, Alabama, Arizona, Arkansas, Colorado, District of Columbia, Hawaii, Idaho, Indiana, Kansas, Kentucky, Louisiana, Maryland, Minnesota, Missouri, Nebraska, New Mexico, Ohio, Oregon, South Carolina, South Dakota, Tennessee, Texas, Utah, Washington, Wisconsin, and Wyoming.

127. *See, e.g.*, Alaska, Arizona, Colorado, Connecticut, Delaware, Florida, Hawaii, Idaho, Illinois, Iowa, Kansas, Kentucky, Louisiana, Maine, Maryland, Massachusetts, Michigan, Mississippi, Missouri, Montana, Nebraska, Nevada, New Hampshire, New Jersey, New Mexico, North Carolina, North Dakota, Oklahoma, Oregon, Pennsylvania, Rhode Island, South Carolina, South Dakota, Tennessee, Texas, Utah, Vermont, Virginia, Washington, and West Virginia.

128. *See, e.g.*, Arkansas, Illinois, and New York.

129. *See, e.g.*, California, District of Columbia, Indiana, New York, Ohio, and Wyoming.

130. *See, e.g.*, Georgia, Minnesota, Texas, and Wisconsin.

131. *See* TENN. CODE ANN. § 37-1-403 (a)(2)(A) (2009).

132. Some states have multiple agencies or vehicles for reporting child abuse. *See, e.g.*, New York.

133. JOHNSON, *supra* note 95, at 55. There is less confusion when the state statute provides for reporting to a state agency rather than local authorities.

134. Social workers should contact their local authorities to determine which of these three options is appropriate in their jurisdiction.

135. TENN. CODE ANN. § 37-1-403 (a)(2)(C),(D).

136. OHIO REV. CODE ANN. § 2151.421 (A)(1)(a).

137. OR. REV. STAT. ANN. § 419B.015 (1)(a).

138. This generally includes the states not listed under the exceptions in the following footnotes. See the Appendix for full details of the individual state statutes.

139. *See, e.g.*, Connecticut.

140. *See, e.g.*, Idaho, Iowa, and Vermont.

141. *See, e.g.*, Kansas, Montana, and Oklahoma.

142. *See, e.g.*, Georgia.

143. *See, e.g.*, Nevada.

144. *See, e.g.*, West Virginia. Texas includes similar language.

145. *See, e.g.*, Washington.

146. *See, e.g.*, Nebraska, North Carolina, Oregon, and South Carolina.

147. *See* JOHNSON, *supra* note 95, at 55.

148. *Id.* at 58. A non-mandatory reporter may refuse to give his or her name. This, however, will not stop the investigation of suspected child abuse. *See, e.g.*, FLA. STAT. ANN. § 39.201 (2)(a)-(c); 325 ILL. COMP. STAT. ANN. 5/7.9.

149. *See, e.g.*, CAL. PENAL CODE § 11167 (e).

150. Unless a court orders the disclosure of information, the identity of the mandated reporter will not be revealed. A mandated reporter's identity may become public information if the reporter is accused of filing a false report or the abuse or neglect case goes to trial. *See* JOHNSON, *supra* note 95, at 58; *see also* FLA. STAT. ANN. § 39.201 (2)(a)-(c).

151. *See, e.g.*, 325 ILL. COMP. STAT. ANN. 5/7 (48 hours); *see also* ARIZ. REV. STAT. ANN. § 13-3620 (A) (West 2010) (72 hours); CAL. PENAL CODE § 11166 (a) (36 hours).

152. *See, e.g.*, DEL. CODE ANN. tit. 16, § 904; D.C. CODE ANN. § 4-1321.03 (a)(2) (2010).

153. *See, e.g.*, ALA. CODE § 26-14-5.

154. MASS. GEN. LAWS ANN. ch. 119, § 51(d) (2010).

155. 980 S.W.2d 278 (Ky. 1998).

156. *Allen*, 980 S.W.2d at 279.

157. *Id.* at 279-80.

158. See, e.g., Alaska, District of Columbia, New York, Oklahoma, Texas, and Wyoming.

159. See, e.g., Georgia, Indiana, Maine, Missouri, Pennsylvania, South Dakota, Tennessee, Virginia, and West Virginia. See also, Hawaii (stating that a staff member must report abuse to the person in charge, who then makes the report to authorities; but does not expressly state that the staff member's obligations have been completed).

160. See, e.g., CAL. PENAL CODE § 11166 (h) ("When two or more persons who are required to report are present and jointly have knowledge of a known or suspected instance of child abuse ... a single report may be made and signed by the selected member of the reporting team.").

161. For a complete examination of privileged communications of social workers, see Carolyn I. Polowy, NATIONAL ASS'N OF SOC. WORKERS, NASW Law Note, Client Confidentiality and Privileged Communications (2011) (identifying the degree that states recognize the social worker–client communication as privileged).

162. Privileged communication is "a legal term that describes the quality of certain specific types of relationships that prevent information, acquired from such relationships, from being disclosed in court or other legal proceedings." P. KEITH-SPIEGEL & G. P. KOOCHER, ETHICS IN PSYCHOLOGY: PROFESSIONAL STANDARDS AND CASES 57 (1985); see also Jaffee v. Redmond, 518 U.S. 1 (1996).

163. See Polowy, supra note 161. See also John Clark, Confidential Communications in a Professional Context: Attorney, Physician, and Social Worker, 24 J. Legal Prof. 79 (2000); DONALD T. DICKSON, CONFIDENTIALITY AND PRIVACY IN SOCIAL WORK: A GUIDE TO THE LAW FOR PRACTITIONERS AND STUDENTS (1998).

164. See In re J.F., 37 P.3d 1227, 1234 (Wash. Ct. App. 2001) (stating "the mandatory reporting requirements ... trump the statutory counselor-patient privilege"); see also Graham vs. United States, 746 A.2d 289, 294–95 (D.C. 2000) (stating "when a mental health provider has made a report to District authorities of suspected child abuse, the trial court may, in its discretion, admit into evidence testimony from that mental health provider as an exception to the mental health provider-patient privilege"); The doctrine of privileged communications, however, continues to be recognized in the course of communications between an attorney and his or her client and, to a lesser degree, in the course of confessions between a penitent to a priest. The attorney–client privilege begins when a client seeks out an individual whom he reasonably believes to be an attorney and divulges private information in seeking professional advice. It is the "client's right to refuse to disclose and to prevent any other person from disclosing confidential communications between the client and the attorney" and permits an attorney to refuse to testify as to communications from client to him though it belongs to client, not to attorney, and hence client may waive it. BLACK'S LAW DICTIONARY (9th ed. 1999), available in WESTLAW.

165. See Polowy, supra note 161.

166. 702 So.2d 825 (La. 1997).

167. Id. at 828.

168. Id. at 831 (noting that the perpetrator signed a waiver of confidentiality form and was able to repeat back to the social worker the substance of the form in his own words.); see also People v. Mineau, 486 N.W.2d 72 (Mich. 1992) (holding that false assurances of confidentiality do not provide protection of the abuser from prosecution, based on other volunteered information).

169. Id. at 832. For a concise overview of child abuse intervention, including the initial report, assessment, and court proceedings, see VERNON R. WIEHE, WORKING WITH CHILD ABUSE AND NEGLECT 83–103 (1996). See also JOHN E. B. MYERS, CHILD PROTECTION IN AMERICA (2006); JOHN E. B. MYERS, LEGAL ISSUES IN CHILD ABUSE AND NEGLECT PRACTICE (2d ed. 1998); DANIEL POLLACK, SOCIAL WORK AND THE COURTS: A CASEBOOK (1997); Robert Schneider, SOCIAL WORK ADVOCACY: A NEW FRAMEWORK FOR ACTION (2000).

170. NATIONAL ASS'N OF SOC. WORKERS, Code of Ethics, Principle 1.07(e) 11 (2008).

171. See H. Foster & D. Freed, Battered Child Legislation and Professional Immunity, 52 A.B.A. J. 1071 (1966).

172. 42 U.S.C. § 5106a (b) (2) (B) (vii).

173. See BESHAROV, supra note 31, at 39.

174. See id.

175. Good faith "A state of mind consisting in (1) honesty in belief or purpose, (2) faithfulness to one's duty or obligation, (3) observance of reasonable commercial standards of fair dealing in a given trade or business, or (4) absence of intent to defraud or to seek unconscionable advantage." BLACK'S LAW DICTIONARY (9th ed. 1999), *available in* WESTLAW.

176. *Cf. Alvarex v. Anesthesiology Ass'n*, 967 S.W.2d 871 (Tex. 1998) (good faith is an issue of fact).

177. *See* BESHAROV, *supra* note 31, at 39. "Rarely is there direct evidence of knowingly false reporting, prejudice, personal bias, or grossly negligent behavior" and, therefore, is very difficult to prove. *See id.* at 41.

178. 1996 WL 39415 (E.D.La., Jan. 30, 1996) (No. CIV. A. 95–969).

179. *Id.* at *4. The Court also acknowledged that "an error in judgment does not constitute bad faith." *Id.*

180. 908 S.W.2d 791 (Mo. 1995).

181. *See id.* at 799; *see also Michaels v. Gordon*, 439 S.E.2d 722, 724 (Ga. 1993); *O'Heron v. Blaney*, 276 Ga. 871, 874 (Ga. 2003); *Maples v. Siddiqui*, 450 N.W.2d 529, 530 (Iowa 1990); *Awkerman v. Tri-county Orthopedic Group, P.C.*, 373 N.W.2d 204, 206 (Mich. 1985); *Lee v. Detroit Medical Center*, 285 Mich. App. 51, 64 (Mich. Ct. App. 2009); *May v. Wyoming Mental Health Ctr.*, 866 P.2d 732, 738 (Wyo. 1993). The court further stated that employers should enjoy the same immunity as their employees. *See D.L.C.*, 908 S.W.2d at 800.

182. 821 P.2d 291 (Ariz. 1991); *see also Ramsey v. Yavapai Family Advocacy Center*, 225 Ariz. 132 (Ariz. Ct. App. 2010).

183. *See id.* at 294–95.

184. *See id.* at 295–96.

185. ARIZ. REV. STAT. ANN. § 13–3620 (G) (2007).

186. *See, e.g.* IDAHO CODE § 16–1606 (2008); IND. CODE ANN. § 31–33–6 (1)-(3) (2007).

187. MONT. CODE ANN. § 41–3–203(1) (2007).

188. *See* Colorado, District of Columbia, Illinois, Indiana, Maine, Michigan, Mississippi, Nevada, New Mexico, New York, North Carolina, North Dakota, Pennsylvania, South Carolina, Tennessee, Wisconsin, and Wyoming.

189. WYO. STAT. ANN. § 14–3–209 (2010).

190. 648 A.2d 53 (Pa. 1994).

191. *See id.* at 477–78; *see also Lehman v. Stephens*, 499 N.E.2d 103 (Ill. 1986) (dismissal appropriate where parents failed to present anything that would rebut statutory presumption); *Gross v. Haight*, 496 So.2d 1225 (La. 1986); *Kempster v. Child Protective Servs.*, 130 A.2d 623 (N.Y. 1987).

192. *See* CAL. PENAL CODE § 11172 (a), (b); OHIO REV. CODE ANN. § 2151.421 (G)(1).

193. Absolute immunity provides a complete bar to recovery by plaintiffs alleging causes of action against a mandatory reporter based on the report given by the reporter. In effect, it is a irrefutable presumption of good faith.

194. OHIO REV. CODE ANN. § 2151.421(G)(1).

195. *See Ferraro v. Chadwick*, 270 Cal. Rptr. 379 (Cal.App. 4 Dist.,1990); *see also Watson v. County of Santa Clara*, 468 F.Supp. 2d 1150 (N.D. Ca. 2007).

196. *See Thomas v. Chadwick*, 274 Cal. Rptr. 128, 133 (1990). Alabama was an "absolute immunity" state, but has since amended its statute to "good faith" immunity. *See Harris v. City of Montgomery*, 435 So.2d 1207 (Ala. 1983); *Brown v. Pound*, 585 So.2d 885 (Ala. 1991) (concluding that when actions are within the mandated requirements, the section provides absolute immunity), *but see* Ala. Code § 26–14–9 (1998) (amending the state statute on immunity to "good faith").

197. 726 N.E.2d 1058 (Ohio Ct. App. 1999).

198. *Id.* at 1064.

199. 529 A.2d 1061 (N.J. Super. Ct. Law Div. 1987).

200. *Id.* at 1063.

201. 45 Cal.Rptr.2d 475 (Cal. 1995); *see also Watson .v County of Santa Clara*, 2007 WL 2471399 (N.D. Ca. 2007).

202. *See id.* at 476.

203. *See id.* at 480. Case law also has made a distinction between discretionary acts and ministerial acts for government workers, finding that the decision to investigate a report (a discretionary act) has qualified immunity, and the act of making sure that the investigation is begun (a ministerial act) has no immunity. *See T.M. v. Noblitt*, 650 So.2d 1340 (Miss. 1995) (holding that public officials have qualified immunity for discretionary conduct, but no immunity for ministerial acts); *see also Thaler v. Child Protective Servs.*, 1998 WL 568302 (Wash.App. Div. 1) (holding that the state may be held liable for a negligent investigation against a parent accused of child abuse). There is also a distinction based on level of service. *See LaShay v. Department of Soc. and Rehab. Serv.*, 625 A.2d 224 (Vt. 1993) (finding that the highest officials should have absolute immunity and lower officials have qualified immunity).

204. *See, e.g.*, Alabama, California, District of Columbia, Florida, Michigan, Pennsylvania, and Texas.

205. *See, e.g.*, Arizona, Connecticut, Idaho, Louisiana, and Virginia.

206. *See* BESHAROV, *supra* note 31, at 30.

207. *See id.* at 29. *See, e.g., Pope v. State*, 382 A.2d 880 (Md. 1978) aff'd in part, rev'd in part, 396 A.2d 1054 (1979).

208. *Cf.* Rudolph Alexander & Cora L. Alexander, *Criminal Prosecution of Child Protection Workers* (Sept. 20, 1993) (unpublished manuscript, on file with the National Association of Social Workers) (detailing several cases in which child care professionals were prosecuted following the death of a child). In *People v. Steinberger*, an unreported case, a social worker was found guilty of official misconduct after an abused child died while under her supervision. *See* Thomas Hafemeister, *Castles Made of Sand? Rediscovering Child Abuse and Society's Response*, 36 Ohio N.U. L. Rev. 819, 863 (2010); LEILA OBIER SCHROEDER, THE LEGAL ENVIRONMENT OF SOCIAL WORK 132 (1995).

209. *See Stevens v. State*, 820 S.W.2d 930 (Tex. 1991).

210. *See id.*

211. *See* JOHNSON, *supra* note 95, at 56.

212. *See* Rudolph Alexander, Jr., *The Legal Liability of Social Workers after DeShaney*, SOCIAL WORK, Jan. 1993, at 64–68 (identifying that the Supreme Court in *DeShaney v. Winnebago County Department of Social Services* restricted civil liability for failure to protect a child under federal law; but suggested that the states may fashion a proper civil remedy through legislation); *see also Professional Liability for Failure to Report Child Abuse*, 38 Am. Jur. Trials 1 (2007).

213. *See, e.g.*, Colorado, Iowa, Montana, and New York.

214. MICH. COMP. LAWS ANN. § 722.633 (1), (2) (West 2010).

215. *See, e.g.*, N.Y. SOC. SERV. LAW § 420 (2).

216. *See* BESHAROV, *supra* note 31, at 31.

217. For a definition of preponderance of the evidence, *see Int'l Seaway Trading Corp. v. Walgreens Corp.*, 599 F.Supp.2d 1307, (S.D. Fla. 2009) (stating "Preponderance of the evidence is established where the evidence weighs, however slightly, in favor of one party over the other"). The preponderance standard is often referred to as "50%+1."

218. *Kansas State Bank & Trust Co. v. Specialized Transp. Serv., Inc.*, 819 P.2d 587, 603 (Kan. 1991); *see also Adams v. Board of Sedwick County Com'rs*, 289 Kan. 577 (Kan. 2009).

219. *See Thelma D. v. Board of Educ. of St. Louis*, 669 F. Supp. 947 (Mo. 1987); *Fischer v. Metcalf*, 543 So.2d 785 (Fla. 1989); *Borne v. Allen County School Corp.*, 532 M.E.2d 1196 (Ind. 1989).

220. 504 N.W.2d 264 (Minn. 1993).

221. *Id.* at 266. *See also Becker v. Mayo Foundation*, 737 N.W.2d 200 (Minn. 2007) (reaffirming that the legislature provided for only criminal, not civil, liability in Minnesota).

222. 819 P.2d 587 (Kan. 1991).

223. *See id.* at 604 (determining that no civil cause of action is created for failure to report suspected child abuse based on criminal misdemeanor, and further that there is no common law principal upon which to rely).

224. *See Landeros v. Flood*, 551 P.2d 389 (Cal. 1976).

225. *See, infra* note 227.

226. *See* 57A Am. Jur. 2d *Negligence* §§ 685–690 (2011).

227. *Alejo v. City of Alhambra*, 89 Cal.Rptr.2d 768 (Cal. Ct. App. 1999).

228. *See, e.g.*, Rowine Brown & Richard Truitt, *Civil Liability in Child Abuse Cases*, 54 Chi.-Kent L. Rev. 753, 760–63 (1978); *see also* Ann Haralambie, *Children's Domestic Tort Claims*, 45 Washburn L.J. 525, 529 (Spring 2006).

229. *See Perry v. S.N.*, 973 S.W.2d 301 (Tex. 1998); *Kansas State Bank & Trust Co. v. Specialized Transp. Serv., Inc.*, 819 P.2d 587 (Kan. 1991). *See also Doe v. Marion*, 645 S.E.2d 245 (S.C. 2007).

230. *See* Black's Law Dictionary (9th ed. 1999), *available in* Westlaw.

231. *See Bentley v. Carroll*, 734 A.2d 697 (Md. 1999) (noting that the violation of the statute was evidence of negligence in the failure to report); *Perry*, 973 S.W.2d 301 (statue as evidence, and not negligence per se).

232. Restatement (Second) of Torts § 314 (1965).

233. Malpractice is "An instance of negligence or incompetence on the part of a professional. To succeed in a malpractice claim, a plaintiff must also prove proximate cause and damages." Black's Law Dictionary (9th ed. 1999), *available in* Westlaw.

234. *See* Besharov, *supra* note 31, at 36; *see also* National Ass'n of Soc. Workers, NASW Standards for Clinical Social Work in Social Work Practice 15–16 (2005).

235. *See Doe v. Maryland. Board of Social Work Examiners*, 384 Md. 161 (Ct. App. Md. 2004).

236. National Ass'n of Soc. Workers, NASW Standards for Clinical Social Work in Social Work Practice 15–16 (2005); for further discussion *see infra* Section on Ethical Considerations.

237. *See, e.g.*, Alabama, Arizona, California, Delaware, Florida, Idaho, Massachusetts, New York, Texas, Virginia, and Washington.

238. Immunity, as discussed above, provides protection to individuals who make a good faith report of suspected child abuse. Immunity does not protect an individual who intentionally makes a false report.

239. *See, e.g.*, Alabama, Colorado, Iowa, Missouri, North Dakota.

240. *See* Fla. Stat. Ann. § 39.205(5) (West Supp. 1999) (3rd degree felony); Tenn. Code Ann. § 37-1-413 (1996) (Class E felony); Tex. Fam. Code Ann. § 261.107 (West 2008). Some states that have misdemeanor classifications, make subsequent false reports felonies. *See, e.g.*, Ark. Code. Ann. §12-18-203 (from Class A misdemeanor to Class D felony).

241. *See* Mich. Comp. Laws Ann. § 722.633 (5)(a)-(b).

242. *See, e.g.*, Connecticut, and Massachusetts.

243. *See* Idaho Code Ann. § 16–1607 (2010); Minn. Stat. Ann. § 626.556 Subd. 5.

244. Colo. Rev. Stat. Ann. § 19–3–304 (3.5)-(4).

245. 325 Ill. Comp. Stat. Ann. 5/4.

246. Frederic G. Reamer, Ethical Standards in Social Work: A Critical Review of the NASW Code of Ethics 54 (2nd Ed. 2006).

247. *See id.* at 57.

248. National Ass'n of Soc. Workers, *Code of Ethics, Principle 1.07(a)* 10 (2008).

249. National Ass'n of Soc. Workers, *Code of Ethics, Principle 1.07(b)* 10 (2008).

250. *See* National Ass'n of Soc. Workers, *Code of Ethics, Principle 1.01 7* (2008).

251. NATIONAL ASS'N OF SOC. WORKERS, *Code of Ethics*, Principle 1.017 (2008); *see also* NATIONAL ASS'N OF SOC. WORKERS, *Current Controversies in Social Work Ethics: Case Examples* 5 (1998).

252. NATIONAL ASS'N OF SOC. WORKERS, *Code of Ethics*, Principle 1.07(c) 10 (2008). This principle also previously stated that confidentiality does not apply "when laws or regulations require disclosure without a client's consent." This portion has since been repealed because of vagueness. When appropriate a social worker should provide information only to the extent necessary and inform the client about the disclosure before it is made. *See id.* at 10–11 (Principle 1.07(d)-(g)); REAMER, *supra* note 246, at 61.

253. Surveys have concluded that the rate of professional noncompliance with mandatory reporting laws is around 60 percent. *See generally* Elizabeth D. Hutchison, *Mandatory Reporting Laws: Child Protective Case Findings Gone Awry?*, SOCIAL WORK, Jan. 1993, at 57; *see also* Douglas J. Besharov & Lisa A. Laumann, *Child Abuse Reporting*, SOC. SCI. & MOD. SOC'Y, May/June 1996, at 40–46. The skill and education of the professional is one factor in determining whether the report will be made and how well it will be made. *See generally* ANTOINETTE A. COLEMAN, CHILD ABUSE REPORTING: AN URBAN PROFILE (1995) (analyzing the differences in reporting between "medical" and "nonmedical" reporters in urban areas).

254. *See* ADMINISTRATION ON CHILDREN, YOUTH AND FAMILIES, UNITED STATES DEPARTMENT OF HEALTH AND HUMAN SERVICES, CHILD MALTREATMENT 2007 8 (2009).

255. *See* NATIONAL CENTER ON CHILD ABUSE AND NEGLECT, U.S. DEP'T OF HEALTH AND HUMAN SERVICES, THE FOURTH NATIONAL INCIDENCE STUDY ON CHILD ABUSE AND NEGLECT 8-3 (2010), *available at* http://www.acf.hhs.gov/programs/opre/abuse_neglect/natl_incid/nis4_report_congress_full_pdf_jan2010.pdf.

256. *See, e.g.*, Douglas J. Besharov, *Ignoring the Danger Signs of Child Abuse*, NEWSDAY, Apr. 21, 1996, at A41; *see also* NATIONAL CENTER ON CHILD ABUSE AND NEGLECT, U.S. DEP'T OF HEALTH AND HUMAN SERVICES, THE FOURTH NATIONAL INCIDENCE STUDY ON CHILD ABUSE AND NEGLECT 8-3 (2010), *available at* http://www.acf.hhs.gov/programs/opre/abuse_neglect/natl_incid/nis4_report_congress_full_pdf_jan2010.pdf; SUSAN ORR, REASON FOUNDATION, CHILD PROTECTION AT THE CROSSROADS: CHILD ABUSE, CHILD PROTECTION, AND RECOMMENDATIONS FOR REFORM 5 (1999). For an examination of the criticisms against child protective services and an understanding of who the critics are, see JOHN E. B. MYERS (ed.), THE BACKLASH: CHILD PROTECTION UNDER FIRE (1994).

257. *See* Gail L. Zellman & Stephen Antler, *Mandated Reporters and CPS: A Study in Frustration*, PUB. WELFARE, Jan. 1993, at 30–37; *see also* MURRAY LEVINE & HOWARD J. DOUECK, THE IMPACT OF MANDATED REPORTING ON THE THERAPEUTIC PROCESS (1995); Robert Lukens, *The Impact of Mandatory Reporting Requirements on the Child Welfare System*, 5 Rutgers J.L. & Pub. Pol'y 177 (Fall 2007). *But see* KALICHMAN, *supra* note 1, at 49–54.

258. *See* JOHNSON, *supra* note 95, at 56.

259. *See, e.g.*, Barry Siegel, *Shadow of Doubt*, L.A. TIMES MAG., Nov. 19, 1989, at 12. The "Johnsons" were accused of abusing their daughter's playmate, and after a three-week intrusive investigation, the allegations were determined to be unsubstantiated. The story focuses on the problem that "once the accusation is made, there is no way to prove guilt and no way to prove innocence." *id.* at 15.

260. *See generally* ORR, *supra* note 256.

261. NATIONAL CENTER ON CHILD ABUSE AND NEGLECT, U.S. DEP'T OF HEALTH AND HUMAN SERVICES, CHILD MALTREATMENT 2009 5–7 (2010), *available at* http://www.acf.hhs.gov/programs/cb/pubs/cm09/index.htm.

262. *Id.*

263. *See, e.g.*, Nolan Rindfleisch & Gerald J. Bean, Jr., *Willingness to Report Abuse and Neglect in Residential Facilities*, 12 CHILD ABUSE & NEGLECT 509, 509–19 (1988); Gail L. Zellman, *Report Decision-Making Patterns among Mandated Child Abuse Reporters*, 14 CHILD ABUSE & NEGLECT 325, 325–35 (1990); Ryan Coulson, *Professional Responsibility and False Accusations of Child Abuse*, 16 J. Contemp. Legal Issues 233 (Fall 2005); M. Meriwether, *Child Abuse Reporting Laws: Time for a Change*, 20 FAM. L. Q. 141, 141–71 (1986); Rebecca Voelker, *Survey: Professionals Fail to Report Suspected Abuse*, AM. MED. ASS'N NEWS, Mar. 2, 1990, at 5.

264. *See, e.g.*, ORR, *supra* note 256; Zellman, *supra* note 263 (believing that the non-functional definitions hinder the professional's ability to report child abuse); Voelker, *supra* note 263.

265. *See* Joan R. Rycraft, *Redefining Abuse & Neglect, A Narrower Focus Could Affect Children at Risk*, PUB. WELFARE, Winter 1990, at 14–21.

266. *See* Voelker, *supra* note 263, at 5.

267. *See* Douglas J. Besharov & Lisa A. Laumann, *Child Abuse Reporting*, Soc. Sci. & Mod. Soc'y, May/June 1996, at 44; *see also* Robert Lukens, *The Impact of Mandatory Reporting Requirements on the Child Welfare System*, 5 Rutgers J.L. & Pub. Pol'y 177 (Fall 2007). *But see* David Finkelhor, *Is Child Abuse Overreported? The Data Rebut Arguments for Less Intervention*, Pub. Welfare, Winter 1990, at 22–29 (arguing that the statistical basis for this recommendation is flawed).

268. *Id.* at 45.

269. *Id.*

270. *See* Orr, *supra* note 256, at 37; *see also* Neil Gilbert (ed.), Combating Child Abuse: International Perspectives and Trends (1997) (identifying alternative designs of child abuse reporting from nine other countries).

271. See, e.g., Cal Penal Code § 11166(j) (requiring an "immediate" or "as soon as practicable" telephonic report, followed up with a written report within 36 hours of receipt of the original report).

272. *Camreta v. Greene*, No. 09-1454, slip op. (U.S. May 26, 2011).

273. *Camreta v. Greene*, No. 09-1454, slip op. (U.S. May 26, 2011).

274. *Greene v. Camreta*, 588 F.3d 1011, 1020 (9th Cir. 2009).

275. *Id.*

276. *Id.* at 1030.

277. *Id.* at 1037.

278. David Hudson, Jr., *What Fourth Amendment Standard Governs In-School Interviews of Children Who May Be Sexual Abuse Victims?* 38 preview of united states supreme court cases 5, 227 (2011). American Bar Association, Division of Public Education. http://www.americanbar.org/content/dam/aba/publishing/previewbriefs/Other_Brief_Updates/aba_preview5_2011.authcheckdam.pdf.

279. *Camreta v. Greene*, 131 S. Ct. 2020 (2011).

280. *Camreta v. Greene*, 131 S. Ct. 2020 (2011).

281. Bernard Pazanowski, *Public Employees' Qualified Immunity No Bar to High Court Review of Underlying Defense*, The U.S. L. Wk., May 31, 2011, at 1.

282. Bernard Pazanowski, *Public Employees' Qualified Immunity No Bar to High Court Review of Underlying Defense*, The U.S. L. Wk., May 31, 2011, at 1, 2.

283. Brief of the National Association of Social Workers, *Camreta* (No. 09-1454).

284. *Franet v. County of Alameda Soc. Servs. Agency*, 291 Fed. Appx. 32 (9th Cir. 2008) (upholding a jury award of $170,000 in compensatory damages against the social worker for the constitutional violation).

285. *Id.* at 35–36.

286. *See, e.g., In re Stumbo*, 582 S.E.2d 255 (N.C. 2003). *Stumbo* reversed a ruling by the Court of Appeals ordering parents not to interfere in the investigation. In this case, investigators were being impeded in their investigation of an anonymous child abuse report of an unsupervised naked toddler outside a home. The parents claimed the investigation was a violation of their Fourth Amendment rights. The court held that because the allegations were not specific enough to meet the definition of a child abuse report under the statute, the investigators had no authority to require parental cooperation in the investigation and a warrant was required.

287. Some jurisdictions have gone so far as to create specific manuals for clergy regarding child abuse reporting. *See* Office of the Attorney General of Alabama, *Child Abuse & Clergy On-line Resource Guide*, http://www.ago.state.al.us/church/ (last visited March 5, 2010).

288. 78 Md. Op. Att'y Gen. 189 (1993).

289. 2001 Ohio Op. Att'y Gen. 2-205, Op. No. 2001-035 (August 2001); 2012 Tex. Op. Att'y. Gen., Op. No. GA-0944 (May 2012).

290. *Baselice v. Franciscan Friars Assumption BVM Province, Inc.*, 879 A.2d 270 (Pa. Super. Ct. 2005).

291. *See* Wash. Rev. Code Ann. § 26.44.030 (2).

292. *Id.*

293. *See* Kathleen Biesterveld, *False Memories and the Public Policy Debate: Toward a Heightened Standard of Care for Psychotherapy*, 2002 Wis. L. Rev. 169 (2002); Colin Gotham, *A Proposed Solution for False Memory Cases: A Gross Negligence Standard*, 8 Kan. J.L. & Pub. Pol'y 205, 205 (1999).

294. *See* Colin Gotham, *A Proposed Solution for False Memory Cases: A Gross Negligence Standard*, 8 Kan. J.L. & Pub. Pol'y 205, 205 (1999).

295. *See Trear v. Sills*, 82 Cal.Rptr.2d 281 (Cal. App. 4 Dist., 1999) (concluding that wrongfully accused father did not have a legal basis for his suit against his daughter's psychologist).

296. *See Franklin v. Stevenson*, 987 P.2d 22 (Utah 1999) (determining that recovered memory testimony was not shown to satisfy foundational requirement of scientific reliability); *see also*, American Bar Ass'n, *Admissibility of Expert Evidence*, 23 Mental & Physical Disability L. Rep. 466, 467 (1999).

297. 42 U.S.C.A. § 16913 (2006).

298. 42 U.S.C. 13031 (1990).

299. 42 U.S.C.A. § 13031(c)(6).

300. 42 U.S.C.A. §13031(c)(1).

301. Definition of sexual explicit conduct includes "actual or simulated sexual intercourse ... or; (v) graphic or simulated lascivious exhibition of the genitals or pubic area of any person." 18 U.S.C.A. 2256(2) (2008).

302. 18 U.S.C.A. 2256 (2008); *see also* 18 U.S.C.A. 1470 (1998); 18 U.S.C.A. 2252 (2008).

303. For example *see* Conn. Gen. Stat. Ann. §53a-193(13) (2005).

304. For example *see* Fla. Stat. Ann. §827.071 (2007); 18 Pa. Cons. Stat. Ann. 6312(d)(2010) (lists possession of child pornography as a form of child sexual abuse).

305. 42 U.S.C.A. 16925 (2006).

306. *See* Feyerick, *Child Pornography: 'Sexting' Lands Teen on Sex Offender List*, CNN, April 07, 2009, *available at* http://articles.cnn.com/2009-04-07/justice/sexting.busts.1_phillip-alpert-offender-list-offender-registry?_s=PM:CRIME; Ziaga, *Federal Child Pornography Law Costing States Real Money*, Legal Match Law Blog, March 2, 2011, *available at* http://lawblog.legalmatch.com/2011/03/02/federal-child-pornography-law-costing-states-real-money/.

307. Child Exploitation and Obscenity Section, U.S. Department of Justice, Child Pornography, http://www.justice.gov/criminal/ceos/subjectareas/childporn.html.

308. Kim, American Prosecutors Research Institute, *From Fantasy to Reality: The Link Between Viewing Child Pornography and Molesting Children*, 1 Child Sexual Exploitation Program Update 3 (2004).

309. Julian Sher & Benedict Carey, *Debate on Child Pornography's Link to Molesting*, N.Y. Times, July 19, 2007, *available at* http://www.nytimes.com/2007/07/19/us/19sex.html?_r=1.

310. *See* Leary, American Prosecutors Research Institute, *Protecting Children from Child Pornography and the Internet: Where Are We Now?* 1 Child Sexual Exploitation Program Update 4 (2004); *see also* McLung, National Center for Prosecution of Child Abuse, *Michigan Supreme Court Rules Copying Child Pornography Images to a CD-ROM Does Not Constitute Production of Child Sexually Abusive Material*, Update Express, Oct. 2010, *available at* http://www.ndaa.org/pdf/Update%20Express%20Oct.%202010.pdf.

311. National Ass'n of Soc. Workers, *Code of Ethics*, Principle 1.07(c) 10 (2008).

312. *USA Saw Lowest Ever Annual Subscriber Growth in 2008*, Cellular-News *available at* http://www.cellular-news.com/story/36734.php?s=h.

313. Amanda Lenhart, Pew Internet and American Life Project [hereinafter Pew Report] 1 (2009), http://pewinternet.org/Reports/2009/Teens-and-Sexting.aspx.

314. Internet World Stats, United States Internet Usage, Broadband, and Telecommunications Reports—Statistics, *available at* http://www.internetworldstats.com/am/us.htm.

315. *See e.g. Online Predators—Child Safety*, MICROSOFT, *available at* http://www.microsoft.com/protect/parents/social/predators.aspx (last visited February 22, 2010); *A Parent's Guide to Internet Safety*, FBI

315. Publications, *available at* http://www.fbi.gov/publications/pguide/pguidee.htm; *To Catch a Predator*, MSNBC, *available at* http://www.msnbc.msn.com/id/10912603 (last visited February 22, 2010).

316. Pew Report, *supra* note 313 at 1.

317. Pew Report, *supra* note 313 at 1.

318. Pew Report, *supra* note 313 at 1.

319. Pew Report, *supra* note 313 at 1.

320. *See supra* section on sexual abuse for definitions.

321. *A.H. v. State*, 946 So.2d 234 (Fla. Dist. Ct. App. 2007) (two teenagers prosecuted for child pornography offenses because A.H. sent sexual picture of herself to her boyfriend); *see also Sexting Leading to Criminal Charges for Teens*, CBS NEWS, Jan. 15, 2009; *Girl Posts Nude Pics is Charged with Kid Porn*, MSNBC.com, Mar. 27, 2009, *available at* http://www.msnbc.msn.com/id/29912729/ (reporting case of 14 year old New Jersey girl facing child pornography cases after posting nude photographs of herself on own Myspace page); *Miller v. Mitchell*, No. 3:09cv540, 2010 WL 1779925 (M.D. Pa. April 30, 2010).

322. 598 F.3d 139 (2010).

323. *Id.* at 152.

324. *See Planned Parenthood Affiliates v. Van De Kamp*, 226 Cal. Rptr. 361 (Cal. Ct. App. 1986) (finding that an Attorney General opinion that construed the mandatory reporter law as requiring reports of consensual sexual acts between minors violated the state constitution); *see also In re G.T.*, 170 Vt. 507 (Vt. 2000).

325. Weronika Kowalczuk, *Abridging Constitutional Rights: Sexting Legislation in Ohio*, 58 Clev. St. L. Rev. 685, 704 (2010); *see also* Clay Calvert, *Sex, Cell Phones, Privacy, and the First Amendment: When Children Become Pornographers and the Lolita Effect Undermines the Law*, 18 CommLaw Conspectus 1 (2009); Meghaan C. McElroy, *Sexual Frustrations: Why the Law Needs to Catch Up to Teenagers' Texts*, 48 Houston Lawyer 10 (2010) (arguing that juvenile sexting should be excluded from child pornography definitions); Jordan J. Szymialis, *Sexting: A Response to Prosecuting Those Growing Up with a Growing Trend*, 44 Ind. L. Rev. 301 (2010) (positing that consensual juvenile sexting should be treated as a juvenile offense requiring rehabilitation and coercive or malicious sexting would require additional penalties).

326. *See* Kim Zetter, *Sexting Hysteria Falsely Brands Educator as Child Pornographer*, WIRE, Apr. 3, 2009, *available at* http://www.wired.com/threatlevel/2009/04/sexting-hysteri/ (assistant principal charged with misdemeanor for failure to report suspected child abuse after confiscation of a picture from student's cell phone); Robert Wood, *The First Amendment Implications of Sexting at Public Schools: A Quandary for Administrators Who Intercept Visual Love Notes*, 18 J.L. & Pol'y 701 (2010).

327. *Logan v. Sycamore Cmty. Sch. Bd. of Educ.*, 2011 U.S. Dist. LEXIS 10505.

328. Jan Hoffman, *States Struggle with Minors' Sexting*, N.Y. Times, March 26, 2011, *available at* http://www.nytimes.com/2011/03/27/us/27sextinglaw.html?ref=us; *see also 2011 legislation Related to "Sexting"*, Nat'l Conf. of State Legs., March 6, 2011, available at http://www.ncsl.org/default.aspx?tabid=22127.

329. For an individualized state overview of the topics discussed in this note, see Appendix.

330. *See* Johnson, *supra* note 95, at 53–61; *see also* American Humane Ass'n, Children's Division, Fact Sheet: Reporting Child Abuse and Neglect, http://www.americanhumane.org/children/stop-child-abuse/fact-sheets/reporting-child-abuse-and-neglect.html (last visited May 19, 2011); Jill Goldman and Marsha Salus, Office on Child Abuse and Neglect, U.S. Dep't of Health and Human Services, A Coordinated Response to Child Abuse and Neglect: The Foundation for Practice 13 (2003) (providing operational definitions for physical abuse, child neglect, sexual abuse, and mental abuse).

331. *See* Michael Weber, *CPS Can't Go It Alone*, Pub. Welfare, Winter 1990, at 18–19.

332. *See* Zellman & Antler, *supra* note 257, at 30–37.

333. *Cf.* Douglas J. Besharov, *Ignoring the Danger Signs of Child Abuse*, Newsday, Apr. 21, 1996, at A41.

*Note:* Endnotes are formatted according to The Bluebook: A Uniform System of Citation (Columbia Law Review Ass'n et al. eds., 18th ed. 2005).

# Appendix A: Individual State Summaries of Mandatory Reporting Requirements 2011[a]

## ALABAMA

**Definitions:** ALA. CODE § 26-14-1(1)-(3) (2003)
**Abuse:** harm or threatened harm to the health or welfare of a child through: (1) non accidental physical injury; (2) non accidental mental injury; (3) sexual abuse or attempted sexual abuse; or (4) sexual exploitation or attempted sexual exploitation.
**Child:** a person under the age of 18 years.
**Neglect:** negligent treatment or maltreatment of a child, including the failure to provide adequate food, clothing, shelter, medical treatment, or supervision.
**Sexual Abuse:** (1) the employment, use, persuasion, inducement, enticement, or coercion of any child to engage in, OR (2) having a child assist any other person to engage in any sexually explicit conduct, OR (3) any simulation of the conduct for the purpose of producing any visual depiction of the conduct; OR (4) the rape, molestation, prostitution, or other form of sexual exploitation of children, OR incest with children.
**Sexual Exploitation:** (1) allowing, permitting, or encouraging a child to engage in prostitution; and (2) allowing, permitting, encouraging, or engaging in the obscene or pornographic photographing, filming, or depicting of a child for commercial purposes.

**Reporting:** ALA. CODE § 26-14-3(a) (2003); § 26-14-10 (2003)
**Who Must Report:** hospitals, clinics, sanitariums, doctors, physicians, surgeons, medical examiners, coroners, dentists, osteopaths, optometrists, chiropractors, podiatrists, nurses, school teachers, and officials; members of clergy; peace officers, law enforcement officials, pharmacists, social workers, day care workers or employees, mental health professionals; any other person called upon to render aid or medical assistance to any child.
**Circumstances:** when the child is known or suspected to be a victim of child abuse or neglect.
**Privileged Communications:** the doctrine of privileged communication, with the exception of the attorney-client privilege, shall not be a ground for excluding any evidence regarding a child's injuries or the case thereof in any judicial proceeding resulting from a report pursuant to this chapter.

**Procedures:** ALA. CODE § 26-14-3(a)-(c) (2004); § 26-14-5 (2008)
**Individual Responsibility:** when the child is known or suspected to be a victim of child abuse or neglect the mandated reporter shall be required to report or cause a report to be made of the same, orally, either by telephone or direct communication immediately, followed by a written report, to a duly constituted authority (chief of police, sheriff, Department of Human Resources, or agency so authorized).
**Contents of Report:** the reports provided for in this chapter shall state, if known: (1) the name of the child, and his whereabouts; (2) the names and addresses of the parents, guardian or caretaker; and (3) the character and extent of his injuries. The written report shall also contain, if known: (1) any evidence of previous injuries to said child; (2) any other pertinent information which might establish the cause of such injury or injuries; and (3) the identity of the person or persons responsible for the same.

---

a  This appendix identifying states' statutes should be used only as a reference guide. It is not a substitute for legal advice or local experts. Most states' statutes are more extensive than space permits here and, although this summary is as current as possible, states' legislatures are continuously modifying the reporting laws.

**Immunity:** ALA. CODE § 26-14-9 (2008)
Any person, firm, corporation or official, including members of a multidisciplinary child protection team, quality assurance team, child death review team, or other authorized case review team or panel, by whatever designation, participating in the making of a good faith report in an investigation or case review authorized under this chapter or other law or department practice or in the removal of a child pursuant to this chapter, or participating in a judicial proceeding resulting there from, shall, in so doing, be immune from any liability, civil or criminal, that might otherwise be incurred or imposed.

**Failure to Report:** ALA. CODE § 26-14-13 (2008)
Any person who knowingly fails to make the report required by the reporting laws shall be guilty of a misdemeanor and shall be punished by a sentence of not more than six months imprisonment or a fine of not more than $500.

**False Reporting:** ALA. CODE § 13A-10-9(a)-(b) (2007)
A person commits the crime of false reporting to law enforcement authorities if he knowingly makes a false report or causes the transmission of a false report to law enforcement authorities of a crime or relating to a crime. False reporting to law enforcement authorities is a Class A misdemeanor.

# ALASKA

**Definitions:** ALASKA STAT. § 47.17.290 (2008)
**Abuse or neglect:** the physical injury or neglect, mental injury, sexual abuse, sexual exploitation, or maltreatment of a child under the age of 18, under circumstances that indicate that the child's health or welfare is harmed or threatened.
**Child:** a person under 18 years of age.
**Maltreatment:** circumstances in which there is reasonable cause to suspect that a child may be in need of aid, due to acts or omissions of a parent, guardian, or custodian, conditions exist that put a child at risk of harm, as described in statute, except that the act or omission need not have been committed by the child's parent, custodian, or guardian.
**Mental Injury:** a serious injury to the child as evidenced by an observable and substantial impairment in the child's ability to function in a developmentally appropriate manner that is supported by the opinion of a qualified expert witness.
**Neglect:** the failure by a person responsible for the child's welfare to provide necessary food, care, clothing, shelter, or medical attention for a child.
**Sexual Exploitation:** allowing a child to engage in prostitution by a person responsible for the child's welfare; or allowing a child to engage in actual or simulated activities of a sexual nature that are prohibited by criminal statute.

**Reporting:** ALASKA STAT. § 47.17.020 (a) (2008); § 47.17.060 (2008)
**Who Must Report:** practitioners of the healing arts; administrative officers of institutions; school teachers, administrative staff members; child care providers; social workers; paid employees of domestic violence and sexual assault programs, and crisis intervention and prevention programs; paid employees of organizations that provide counseling or treatment to individuals seeking to control their use of drugs or alcohol; licensed marital and family therapists; peace officers; officers of the Department of Corrections; persons who process or produce visual or printed matter, either privately or commercially; members of a child fatality review team or the multidisciplinary child protection team.
**Circumstances:** when, in the performance of their occupational duties or appointed duties, they have reasonable cause to suspect that a child has suffered harm as a result of child abuse or neglect.
**Privileged Communications:** neither the physician-patient nor the husband-wife privilege is a ground for excluding evidence regarding a child's harm, or its cause, in a judicial proceeding related to a report made under the reporting statute.

**Procedures:** ALASKA STAT. § 47.17.020
**Individual Responsibility:** a) In the performance of their occupational duties, or their appointed duties, if mandated reporters have reasonable cause to suspect that a child has suffered harm as a result of child abuse or neglect, they shall immediately report the harm to the nearest office of the department.

**Immunity:** Alaska Stat. § 47.17.050 (2008)
Except as provided below, a person who, in good faith, makes a report under the reporting laws, permits an interview, or participates in judicial proceedings related to submission of reports, is immune from civil or criminal liability that might otherwise be incurred or imposed for making the report or permitting the interview, except that a person who knowingly makes an untimely report is not immune from civil or criminal liability based on the delay in making the report.
A person accused of committing the child abuse or neglect is not immune from civil or criminal liability for the child abuse or neglect as a result of reporting the child abuse or neglect.

**Failure to Report:** Alaska Stat. § 47.17.068 (2006)
A person who fails to comply with the laws requiring reports of child abuse or neglect or child pornography and who knew or should have known that the circumstances gave rise to the need for a report, is guilty of a Class A misdemeanor.

**False Reporting:**
Not specifically addressed in statute.

# ARIZONA

**Definitions:** Ariz. Rev. Stat. Ann. § 8-201(1), (2), (6), (8), (13)(a)(I)-(ii), (21) (2008)
**Abandoned:** failure of a parent to provide reasonable support and to maintain regular contact with the child, including providing normal supervision. 'Abandoned' includes a judicial finding that a parent has made only minimal efforts to support and communicate with the child. Failure to maintain a normal parental relationship with the child without just cause for a period of six months constitutes prima facie evidence of abandonment.
**Abuse:** the infliction or allowing of physical injury, impairment of bodily function or disfigurement or the infliction of or allowing another person to cause serious emotional damage as evidenced by severe anxiety, depression, withdrawal, or untoward aggressive behavior and which emotional damage is diagnosed by a medical doctor or psychologist and which is caused by the acts or omissions of an individual having care, custody, and control of a child. Abuse shall include inflicting or allowing sexual abuse, sexual conduct with a minor, sexual assault, molestation of a child, commercial sexual exploitation of a minor, incest; or child prostitution.
**Child, Youth, or Juvenile:** an individual who is under the age of 18 years.
**Neglect:** means the inability or unwillingness of a parent, guardian or custodian of a child to provide that child with supervision, food, clothing, shelter or medical care if that inability or unwillingness causes substantial risk of harm to the child's health or welfare, except if the inability of a parent or guardian to provide services to meet the needs of a child with a disability or chronic illness is solely the result of the unavailability of reasonable services.

**Reporting:** Ariz. Rev. Stat. Ann. § 13-3620 (A), (C) (2003); § 8-805 (B), (C) (2008)
**Who Must Report:** physicians, hospital interns or residents, surgeons, dentists, osteopaths, chiropractors, podiatrists, county medical examiners, nurses, psychologists, school personnel, social workers, peace officers, parents, counselors, clergymen, priests, or any other person having responsibility for the care or treatment of children.
**Circumstances:** when observation or examination of any minor discloses reasonable grounds to believe that a minor is or has been the victim of injury, sexual abuse, incest, child prostitution, death, abuse, physical neglect which appears to have been inflicted by other than accidental means or not explained by available medical history as being accidental in nature, or denial or deprivation of necessary medical treatment or surgical care or nourishment with the intent to cause or allow the death of an infant less than one year of age.
**Privileged Communications:** the physician-patient privilege, husband-wife privilege, or any privilege except the attorney-client privilege, provided for by professions such as social work shall not pertain in any civil or criminal litigation. A clergyman or priest who has received a confidential communication or confession in that person's role as priest may withhold reporting if he determines that it is reasonable and necessary within the concepts of the religion. This exemption applies only to communications and not to personal observations he may otherwise make.

Appendix A

**Procedures:** Ariz. Rev. Stat. Ann. § 13-3620 (A), (E), (F) (2007)
**Individual Responsibility:** any mandated reporter or any other person having responsibility for the care or treatment of children whose observation or examination of any minor discloses reasonable grounds to believe that a minor is or has been the victim of [listed forms of abuse and neglect], shall immediately report or cause reports to be made of this information to a peace officer or to child protective services in the Department of Economic Security.
**Content of Report:** Reports shall be made forthwith by telephone or in person forthwith and shall be followed by a written report within 72 hours. The reports shall contain names and addresses of the minor and the minor's parents or the person or persons having custody of the minor, if known; minor's age and nature and extent of minor's injuries or physical neglect, including any evidence of previous injuries or physical neglect, and any other information that the person believes might be helpful in establishing the cause of the injury or physical neglect.

**Immunity:** Ariz. Rev. Stat. Ann. § 13-3620 (G) (2007); § 8-805 (A) (2008)
   A person furnishing a report, information, or records required or authorized under this section, or a person participating in a judicial or administrative proceeding or investigation resulting from a report, information or records required or authorized under this section, shall be immune from any civil or criminal liability by reason of such actions unless the person acted with malice or unless the person has been charged with or is suspected of abusing or neglecting the child or children in question.

**Failure to Report:** Ariz. Rev. Stat. Ann. § 13-3620(O); §13-3620(P)(4); §13-3506.01(A) (2008)
   A person who violates this section is guilty of a class 1 misdemeanor, except if the failure to report involves a reportable offense, the person is guilty of a class 6 felony.
**Reportable offense:** Incest, child prostitution, surreptitious photographing, videotaping, filming or digitally recording (any person, with knowledge of the character of the item involved, to intentionally or knowingly transmit or send to a minor by means of electronic mail, personal messaging or any other direct internet communication an item that is harmful to minors when the person knows or believes at the time of the transmission that a minor in this state will receive the item.

**False Reporting:** Ariz. Rev. Stat. Ann. § 13-3620.01 (A), (B) (2008)
   A person acting with malice who knowingly and intentionally makes a false report of child abuse or neglect, or a person acting with malice who coerces another person to make a false report of child abuse or neglect, is guilty of a Class 1 misdemeanor.
   A person who knowingly and intentionally makes a false report that another person made a false report is guilty of a Class 1 misdemeanor.

# ARKANSAS

**Definitions:** Ark. Code Ann. §12-18-103 (2011)
**Abandonment:** means (i) The failure of a parent to provide reasonable support and to maintain regular contact with a child through statement or contact when the failure is accompanied by an intention on the part of the parent to permit the condition to continue for an indefinite period in the future or the failure of a parent to support or maintain regular contact with a child without just cause; or (ii) An articulated intent to forego parental responsibility.
  (B) "Abandonment" does not include acts or omissions of a parent toward a married minor;
**Abuse:** (A) means any of the following acts or omissions by a parent, guardian, custodian, foster parent, person eighteen (18) years of age or older living in the home with a child whether related or unrelated to the child, or any person who is entrusted with the child's care by a parent, guardian, custodian, or foster parent, including, but not limited to, an agent or employee of a public or private residential home, child care facility, public or private school, or any person legally responsible for the child's welfare, but excluding the spouse of a minor:
   (i) Extreme or repeated cruelty to a child;
   (ii) Engaging in conduct creating a realistic and serious threat of death, permanent or temporary disfigurement, or impairment of any bodily organ;
   (iii) Injury to a child's intellectual, emotional, or psychological development as evidenced by observable and substantial impairment of the child's ability to function within the child's normal range of performance and behavior;
   (iv) Any injury that is at variance with the history given;

(v) Any non-accidental physical injury;
(vi) Any of the following intentional or knowing acts, with physical injury and without justifiable cause:
   (a) Throwing, kicking, burning, biting, or cutting a child;
   (b) Striking a child with a closed fist;
   (c) Shaking a child; or
   (d) Striking a child on the face or head; or
(vii) Any of the following intentional or knowing acts, with or without physical injury:
   (a) Striking a child six (6) years of age or younger on the face or head;
   (b) Shaking a child three (3) years of age or younger;
   (c) Interfering with a child's breathing;
   (d) Pinching, biting, or striking a child in the genital area;
   (e) Tying a child to a fixed or heavy object or binding or tying a child's limbs together;
   (f) Giving a child or permitting a child to consume or inhale a poisonous or noxious substance not prescribed by a physician that has the capacity to interfere with normal physiological functions;
   (g) Giving a child or permitting a child to consume or inhale a substance not prescribed by a physician that has the capacity to alter the mood of the child, including, but not limited to, the following: (1) Marijuana; (2) Alcohol, excluding alcohol given to a child during a recognized and established religious ceremony or service; (3) A narcotic; or (4) An over-the-counter drug if a person purposely administers an overdose to a child or purposely gives an inappropriate over-the-counter drug to a child and the child is detrimentally impacted by the overdose or the over-the-counter drug;
   (h) Exposing a child to a chemical that has the capacity to interfere with normal physiological functions, including, but not limited to, a chemical used or generated during the manufacture of methamphetamine; or (i) Subjecting a child to Munchausen syndrome by proxy or a factitious illness by proxy if the incident is confirmed by medical personnel.
(B)(i) The list in subdivision (2)(A) of this section is illustrative of unreasonable action and is not intended to be exclusive.
(ii) No unreasonable action shall be construed to permit a finding of abuse without having established the elements of abuse.
(C)(i) "Abuse" does not include physical discipline of a child when it is reasonable and moderate and is inflicted by a parent or guardian for purposes of restraining or correcting the child.
(ii) "Abuse" does not include when a child suffers transient pain or minor temporary marks as the result of an appropriate restraint if: (a) The person exercising the restraint is: (1) An employee of a child welfare agency licensed or exempted from licensure under the Child Welfare Agency Licensing Act, § 9-28-401 et seq.; and (2) Acting in his or her official capacity while on duty at a child welfare agency licensed or exempted from licensure under the Child Welfare Agency Licensing Act, § 9-28-401 et seq.; ...
(iii) Reasonable and moderate physical discipline inflicted by a parent or guardian does not include any act that is likely to cause and which does cause injury more serious than transient pain or minor temporary marks.
(iv) The age, size, and condition of the child and the location of the injury and the frequency or recurrence of injuries shall be considered when determining whether the physical discipline is reasonable or moderate.

**Child or Juvenile:** means an individual who is from birth to eighteen (18) years of age.
**Neglect:** failure or refusal to prevent abuse; provide necessary food, clothing, shelter, and education or medical treatment (unless financially unable); or protect juvenile from child maltreatment.
(B)(i) "Neglect" shall also include:
   (a) Causing a child to be born with an illegal substance present in the child's bodily fluids or bodily substances as a result of the pregnant mother's knowingly using an illegal substance before the birth of the child; or
   (b) At the time of the birth of a child, the presence of an illegal substance in the mother's bodily fluids or bodily substances as a result of the pregnant mother's knowingly using an illegal substance before the birth of the child.
**Sexual Abuse:** solicitation or participation in sexual activity with a juvenile by a person responsible for the child's care.

**Reporting:** Ark. Code Ann. § 12-18-402 (2011)
**Who Must Report:** physicians; surgeons; coroners; dentists; osteopaths; resident interns; licensed nurses; medical personnel who may be engaged in admission, examination, care, or treatment of persons; teachers; school officials; school counselors; day-care center workers; social workers; family service workers; mental health professionals; any other child or foster care workers; peace officers; law enforcement officials; prosecuting attorneys; and judges; and others.
**Circumstances:** when they have reasonable cause to suspect that a child has been subjected to, or died as a result of, child maltreatment; when they have observed the child being subjected to conditions or circumstances that would reasonably result in child maltreatment.
**Privileged Communications:** no privilege or contract shall relieve any mandatory reporter of this responsibility.

**Procedures:** Ark. Code Ann. § 12-18-402 (2011)
**Individual Responsibility:** when any mandated reporter has reasonable cause to suspect that a child has been subjected to child maltreatment, or that a child has died as a result of child maltreatment, or who observes the child being subjected to conditions or circumstances that would reasonably result in child maltreatment, he shall immediately notify the child abuse hotline.

**Immunity:** Ark. Code Ann. § 12-18-107 (2009)
Any person or agency required to participate and acting in good faith in making notification or taking photographs or X-rays or the removal of a child while exercising protective services, shall be immune to suit and to liability, both civil and criminal.
All other persons making notification, if acting in good faith, shall be immune from liability.

**Failure to Report:** Ark. Code Ann. §§ 12-18-201, 12-18-202 (2009)
Failure to notify by a mandated reporter in the first degree is a Class A misdemeanor, when a mandated reporter with reasonable cause to suspect that a child has been subjected to child maltreatment; or has died as a result of child maltreatment; or observes a child being subjected to conditions or circumstances that would reasonably result in child maltreatment; and knowingly fails to notify the Child Abuse Hotline of the child maltreatment or suspected child maltreatment.
A person commits the offense of failure to notify by a mandated reporter in the second degree if he or she:
(1) Is a mandated reporter under this chapter;
(2) Has:
 (A) Reasonable cause to suspect that a child has been subjected to child maltreatment;
 (B) Reasonable cause to suspect that a child has died as a result of child maltreatment; or
 (C) Observes a child being subjected to conditions or circumstances that would reasonably result in child maltreatment; and
(3) Recklessly fails to notify the Child Abuse Hotline of the child maltreatment or suspected child maltreatment.
(b) Failure to notify by a mandated reporter in the second degree is a Class C misdemeanor.

**False Reporting:** Ark. Code Ann. §12-18-203(a)
A person commits the offense of making a false report under this chapter if he or she purposely makes a report containing a false allegation to the Child Abuse Hotline knowing the allegation to be false.
(b)(1) A first offense of making a false report under this chapter is a Class A misdemeanor.
(2) A subsequent offense of making a false report under this chapter is a Class D felony.

# CALIFORNIA

**Definitions:** Cal. Penal Code § 11165.1 (2008); § 11165.2 (West 1992); § 11165.3 (2007); §§ 11165.4–.6 (2008)

**Abuse:** any physical injury which is inflicted by other than accidental means on a child by another person, and includes generally other definitions listed in this section. (Abuse in out-of-home care is abuse of a child by a facility licensed to care for children, employee of a public or private school, or other agency.)

**Neglect:** the negligent treatment or maltreatment of a child by a person responsible for the child's welfare under circumstances indicating harm or threatened harm to the child's health (includes "severe" and "general" definitions).

**Sexual Abuse:** sexual assault (including rape, statutory rape, rape in concert, incest, sodomy, lewd or lascivious acts upon a child, oral copulation, penetration of a genital or anal opening by a foreign object, or molestation [illustrative list]), or sexual exploitation (involving depicting a minor engaged in obscene acts in violation of law; any person who knowingly promotes, aids, or assists a child in prostitution or performance involving obscene conduct, or to pose or model).

**Willful Harming or Endangering a Child:** a situation where any person willfully causes or permits any child to suffer, or inflicts thereon, unjustifiable physical pain or mental suffering, or willfully causes or permits the person or health of the child to be placed in a situation such that his or her person or health is endangered.

**Reporting:** Cal. Penal Code § 11166 (a), (c), (e) (West Supp. 1998); § 11165.7 (a)–.8 (2008); § 11166(e) (2007)

**Who Must Report:** physician, surgeon, psychiatrist/psychologist or assistant, dentist/hygienist, resident/intern, podiatrist, chiropractor, licensed nurse, optometrist, marriage/child counselor or trainee, emergency technician/paramedic, health employee treating minors for venereal diseases, coroner; teacher, instructional/teacher's aide or employed assistant, employee of any public school, any officer/supervisor of child welfare, certificated pupil personnel, administrator/worker of public or private child agency, administrator/employee of licensed community/child day care, Headstart, social worker, probation/parole officer, school police/security department, counselor of child abuse, D.A. investigator, inspector, family support/peace officer; C.P.S. employee, visitation monitor, firefighter, animal control, humane safety officer, film/print processors, clergy, law officers.

**Circumstances:** when they have knowledge of or observe a child, in their professional capacity or in the scope of employment, who they know or reasonably suspect has been the victim of child abuse, has been inflicted with mental suffering or the child's well-being is endangered.

**Privileged Communications:** a clergy member who acquires knowledge or reasonable suspicion of child abuse during penitential communication is not subject to these requirements, but is when acting in other capacities.

**Procedures:** Cal. Penal Code § 11166 (a)-(c), (e)-(i) (2007); § 11167 (a), (e) (2007); § 11168 (2007)

**Individual Responsibility:** except as provided below, any mandated reporter who has knowledge of or observes a child, in his or her professional capacity or in the scope of his or her employment, who he or she knows or reasonably suspects has been the victim of child abuse, shall report the know or suspected instance of child abuse to a child protective agency immediately or as soon as practically possible by telephone and shall prepare and send a written report thereof within 36 hours of receiving the information concerning the incident.

Any other person who has knowledge of or observes a child who he or she knows or reasonably suspects has been a victim of child abuse may report the known or suspected instance of child abuse to a child protective agency.

**Content of Report:** a telephone report of a known or suspected instance of child abuse shall include the name of the person making the report; the name of the child, the present location of the child; the nature and extent of injuries; and any other information, including what led that person to suspect child abuse, requested by the child protective agency.

Written reports required by the reporting laws shall be submitted on forms adopted by the Department of Justice. Such forms shall be distributed by the child protective agencies.

**Immunity:** CAL. PENAL CODE § 11172 (a), (b) (2008)
A mandatory reporter who reports a known or suspected instance of child abuse shall not be civilly or criminally liable for any report required or authorized by law.
Any other person reporting a known or suspected instance of child abuse shall not incur civil or criminal liability as a result of any report authorized by law, unless it can be proven that a false report was made and the person knew that the report was false or was made with reckless disregard of the truth or falsity of the report.
No mandatory reporter, nor any person taking photographs at his or her direction, shall incur any civil or criminal liability for taking photographs of a suspected victim of child abuse, without parental consent, or for disseminating the photographs with the reports required by law. This section does not grant immunity from liability with respect to any other use of the photographs.
Any mandatory reporter who, pursuant to a request from a child protective agency, provides the requesting agency with access to the victim of known or suspected instance of child abuse shall not incur civil or criminal liability as a result of providing that access.

**Failure to Report:** CAL. PENAL CODE § 11162; 11166.01 (2007)
Any mandatory reporter who violates this section shall be punished by not more than six months in a county jail, by a fine of not more than one thousand dollars ($1,000), or by both fine and imprisonment.
Any mandated reporter who willfully fails to report abuse or neglect, or any person who impedes or inhibits a report of abuse or neglect, in violation of this article, where that abuse or neglect results in death or great bodily injury, shall be punished by not more than one year in a county jail, by a fine of not more than five thousand dollars ($5,000), or by both that fine and imprisonment.

**False Reporting:** CAL. PENAL CODE § 11172 (a) (2008)
Any other person reporting a known or suspected instance of child abuse shall not incur civil or criminal liability as a result of any report authorized by this article unless it can be proven that a false report was made and the person knew that the report was false or was made with reckless disregard of the truth of falsity of the report, and any person who makes a report of child abuse known to be false or with reckless disregard of the truth or falsity of the report is liable for any damages caused.

# COLORADO

**Definitions:** COLO. REV. STAT. ANN. § 19-1-103
**Abuse or Neglect:** an act or omission that threatens the health or welfare of a child: skin bruising or bleeding, malnutrition, failure to thrive, bone fractures, swelling, death not product of accident or justifiably explained; sexual assault or molestation; failure to provide adequate basic needs; emotional abuse; neglect.
**Emotional Abuse:** an identifiable and substantial impairment, or risk of impairment, of the child's intellectual or psychological functioning or development.
**Institutional Abuse:** any case of abuse that occurs in any public or private facility in the state that provides child care out of the home, supervision, or maintenance.
**Neglected or Dependent:** abandonment, mistreatment, or abuse by parent/guardian or allowing another to mistreat child w/o taking lawful steps to stop; lacking proper care; living in an injurious environment; refused proper subsistence, education, medical care; homeless or run-away. Also includes any conduct falling under "abuse/neglect".
**Sexual Conduct:** sexual intercourse (in any fashion between humans or humans and animals), penetration of vagina or rectum by any object, masturbation, or sadomasochistic abuse.

**Reporting:** COLO. REV. STAT. ANN. § 19-3-304 (1), (2), (2.5) (2008); § 19-3-311 (2008)
**Who Must Report:** physician, surgeon, physician in training, child health associates, medical examiners/coroners, dentists, osteopaths, optometrists, chiropractors, podiatrists, registered nurses, licensed practical nurses, hospital admissions, care or treatment personnel, hygienists, physical therapists, pharmacists; public/private school officials/employees, workers in family care/foster care homes, or child centers; social workers, Christian Science practitioners, mental health professionals, psychologists; veterinarians, peace officers/firemen, victim's advocates; commercial film and photographic print processors.
**Circumstances:** when they have reasonable cause to know or suspect that a child is subject to abuse or neglect; have observed circumstances or conditions that would reasonably result in abuse or neglect; observed or have knowledge of any film or photograph depicting a child engaged in an act of sexual conduct (for film and print processors in their professional capacity).
**Privileged Communications:** no patient–physician, patient–professional nurse, school psychologist–client, or husband–wife privilege will exclude evidence resulting from the reporting of abuse.

**Procedures:** COLO. REV. STAT. ANN. § 19-3-304 (1), (2.5) (2008); § 19-3-307 (1)-(3) (2008)
**Individual Responsibility:** except as provided below, any mandated reporter who has reasonable cause to know or suspect that a child has been subjected to abuse or neglect or who has observed the child being subjected to circumstances or conditions that would reasonably result in abuse or neglect shall immediately report or cause a report to be made of such fact to the county Department of Social Services or local law enforcement agency.
**Content of Report:** when possible, reports shall include name, address, age, sex, and race of child; name and address of person suspected of the abuse; nature and extent of child injuries, including any evidence of previous abuse; family composition; source or report; name, address, and occupation of person making report; any action taken by reporting source; any other helpful information.

**Immunity:** COLO. REV. STAT. ANN. § 19-3-309 (2008)
Any person, other than the perpetrator, complicitor, coconspirator, or accessory, participating in good faith in the making of a report pursuant to the reporting laws, in the facilitation of the investigation of such a report, in a judicial proceeding resulting there from, or in the taking of photographs or x-rays, or the placing in temporary protective custody of a child, or otherwise performing his duties or acting pursuant to law, shall be immune from any civil or criminal liability or termination of employment that otherwise might result by reason of such acts of participation, unless a court of competent jurisdiction determines that such person's behavior was willful, wanton, and malicious.
For the purpose of any civil or criminal proceedings, the good faith of any such person reporting child abuse, any such person taking photographs or x-rays, and any such person who has legal authority to place a child in protective custody, shall be presumed.

**Failure to Report:** COLO. REV. STAT. ANN. § 19-3-304 (4) (2008)
Any person who willfully violates the provisions of the reporting laws commits a Class 3 misdemeanor and shall be punished as provided by law and shall be liable for damages proximately caused thereby.

**False Reporting:** COLO. REV. STAT. ANN. § 19-3-304 (3.5), (4) (2008)
No person, including a mandatory reporter, shall knowingly make a false report of abuse or neglect to a county department or local law enforcement agency. Any person who violates this provision commits a Class 3 misdemeanor and shall be punished as provided by law and shall be liable for damages proximately caused thereby.

# CONNECTICUT

**Definitions:** Conn. Gen. Stat. Ann. § 46b-120 (2012)
**Abused:** means that a child or youth has had physical injury or injuries inflicted other than by accident, or has injuries that are at variance with the history given them, or is in a condition of maltreatment (malnutrition, sexual molestation or exploitation, deprivation of necessities, emotional maltreatment or cruel punishment).
**Child:** any person under 18 years of age, who has not been emancipated.
**Neglected Child:** a child or youth who has been abandoned or is being denied proper care and attention (physically, educationally, emotionally, or morally) or is being permitted to live in conditions or circumstances that are injurious or has been abused.
**Uncared For Child:** a child or youth who is homeless, or whose home cannot provide the care that his/her physical, emotional, or mental condition requires.
**Youth:** any person 16 to 19 years of age who has not been legally emancipated.

**Reporting:** Conn. Gen. Stat. Ann. § 17a-101 (2010)
**Who Must Report:** licensed physician or surgeon, resident physician or intern in any hospital; registered nurse, licensed practical nurse, medical examiner, dentist, hygienist; physician assistant, pharmacist, physical therapist, osteopath, optometrist, chiropractor, podiatrist; psychologist, mental health professional; school teacher, principal, guidance counselor, school paraprofessional; social worker, police officer, clergyman, licensed substance abuse counselor, licensed marital family therapist, sexual assault counselor, battered women's counselor, or any person paid to care for a child in any public/private facility, day care center or family day care home which is licensed by the state.
**Circumstances:** when any mandated reporter, in his professional capacity, has reasonable cause to suspect or believe that any child under 18 has been abused.

**Procedures:** Conn. Gen. Stat. Ann. §§ 17–101a- 17–101d (2003)
**Individual Responsibility:** any mandated reporter who has reasonable cause to suspect or believe that a child has been abused shall report or cause a report to be made in accordance with reporting procedures. An oral report shall be made within 12 hours of having reasonable cause to suspect or believe that a child has been abused, by telephone or in person to the Commissioner of Children and Families or a law enforcement agency. When suspected abuser is a staff member of a public/private institution that provides child care, reporter shall also notify the person in charge. Within 48 hours of making an oral report, a mandate reporter shall submit a written report to the Commissioner.
**Content of Report:** all oral and written reports shall contain, if known, names and addresses of the child and parents/guardians; age and gender of child, nature and extent of injuries/maltreatment; approximate date and time of injury; information of any previous maltreatment; circumstances of injury; name of person suspected of causing injury; and whatever action, if any, taken to assist the child.

**Immunity:** Conn. Gen. Stat. Ann. § 17a-101e (b) (2008)
Any person, institution or agency which, in good faith, makes or in good faith does not make a report shall be immune from any liability, civil or criminal, which might otherwise be incurred or imposed and shall have the same immunity with respect to any judicial proceeding which results from such report provided such person did not perpetrate or cause such abuse or neglect.

**Failure to Report:** Conn. Gen. Stat. Ann. § 17a-101a (2002)
Any person required to report under the provisions of this section who fails to make such report shall be fined not less than five hundred dollars or more than two thousand five hundred dollars and shall be required to participate in an educational and training program.

**False Reporting:** Conn. Gen. Stat. Ann. § 17a-101e (c) (2008)
Any person who knowingly makes a false report of child abuse or neglect shall be fined not more than $2,000 or imprisoned not more than one year, or both.

# DELAWARE

**Definitions:** Del. Code Ann. tit. 16, § 902 (2004)
**Abuse:** any physical injury to a child by those responsible for the care, custody and control of the child through unjustified force, emotional abuse, torture, criminally negligent treatment, sexual abuse, exploitation, maltreatment, or mistreatment.
**Child:** any person who has not reached his or her 18th birthday.
**Neglect:** the failure to provide, by those responsible for the care, custody, and control of the child, the proper or necessary education as required by law; nutrition; or medical, surgical, or any other care necessary for the child's well-being; chronically and severely abuses alcohol or a controlled substance, is not active in treatment for such abuse, and the abuse threatens the child's ability to receive care necessary for that child's general well-being; fails to provide necessary supervision appropriate for a child when the child is unable to care for that child's own basic needs or safety, after considering such factors as the child's age, mental ability, physical condition, the length of the caretaker's absence, and the context of the child's environment. In making a finding of neglect under this section, consideration may be given to dependency, neglect, or abuse history of any party.

**Reporting:** Del. Code Ann. tit. 16, § 903 (2008); § 909 (2008)
**Who Must Report:** physicians; any other persons in the healing arts, including persons licensed to render services in medicine, osteopathy, or dentistry; interns; residents; nurses; medical examiners; school employees; social workers; psychologists; any other persons.
**Circumstances:** when they know or in good faith suspect child abuse or neglect.
**Privileged Communications:** no legally recognized privilege, except that between attorney and client and that between priest and penitent in a sacramental confession, shall apply to situations involving known or suspected child abuse, neglect, exploitation, or abandonment and shall not constitute grounds for failure to report as required or to give or accept evidence in any judicial proceeding relation to child abuse or neglect.

**Procedures:** Del. Code Ann. tit. 16, § 904 (2008)
**Individual Responsibility:** any report required to be made under this chapter shall be made to the Division of Child Protective Services of the Department of Services for Children, Youth and Their Families. An immediate oral report shall be made by telephone or otherwise. A written report shall be made if requested.
**Content of Report:** reports and the contents thereof, including a written report, if requested, shall be made in accordance with the rules and regulations of the Division of Child Protective Services or in accordance with the rules and regulations adopted by the Division.

**Immunity:** Del. Code Ann. tit. 16, § 908 (2008)
Anyone participating in good faith in the making of a report, performing a medical examination without the consent of those responsible for the care, custody, and control of the child, or exercising emergency protective custody in compliance with provisions of this chapter, shall have immunity from any liability, civil or criminal, that might otherwise exist, and such immunity shall extend to participation in any judicial proceedings resulting from the above actions taken in good faith. This section shall not limit the liability of any health care provider for personal injury claims due to medical negligence that occurs as a result of any examination performed pursuant to this statute.

**Failure to Report:** Del. Code Ann. tit. 16, § 914 (2008)
(a) Whoever violates § 903 of this title shall be liable for a civil penalty not to exceed $10,000 for the first violation, and not to exceed $50,000 for any subsequent violation.
(b) In any action brought under this section, if the court finds a violation, the court may award costs and attorneys' fees.

**False Reporting:** Del. Code Ann. tit. 16, § 914 (2008)
(a) Whoever violates § 903 of this title shall be liable for a civil penalty not to exceed $10,000 for the first violation, and not to exceed $50,000 for any subsequent violation.
(b) In any action brought under this section, if the court finds a violation, the court may award costs and attorneys' fees.

# DISTRICT OF COLUMBIA

**Definitions:** D.C. Code Ann. § 16–2301 (9), (23)-(25) (2010)
**Abused Child:** a child whose parent, guardian, or custodian inflicts or fails to make reasonable efforts to prevent the infliction of physical or mental injury upon the child, including excessive corporal punishment, sexual abuse, molestation, or exploitation or an injury that results from exposure to drug-related activity in the child's home environment.
**Neglected Child:** a child who has been abandoned or abused by his or her parent, guardian, or custodian (including the parent's inability to assume responsibility due to incarceration, hospitalization, or other physical or mental incapacity); is without proper parental care, subsistence education or other care or control for physical, mental, or emotional needs; is in imminent danger of being abused and whose sibling has been abused; has received negligent treatment; or has resided in a D.C. hospital for at least 10 days after birth, despite being ready for discharge and parent has not taken any action to maintain a relationship with the child.
**Negligent Treatment:** failure to provide adequate food, clothing, shelter, or medical care, and the deprivation is not due to the lack of financial means of parent, guardian, or custodian.
**Sexual Exploitation:** a parent, guardian, or custodian allows a child to engage in prostitution or obscene/pornographic photography or filming or promotes sexual conduct.

**Reporting:** D.C. Code Ann. §4–1321.02–.05
**Who Must Report:** a physician, psychologist, medical examiner, dentist, chiropractor, registered nurse, licensed practical nurse, person involved in the care and treatment of patients, law-enforcement officer, humane officer of any agency charged with the enforcement of animal cruelty laws, school official, teacher, athletic coach, Department of Parks and Recreation employee, public housing resident manager, social service worker, day care worker, human trafficking counselor as defined in § 14–311(2), domestic violence counselor as defined in § 14–310(a)(2), and mental health professional as defined in § 7–1201.01(11).
**Circumstances:** when they know have reasonable cause to suspect that a child known to him or her in his or her professional or official capacity has been or is in immediate danger of being a mentally or physically abused or neglected child, as defined in § 16–2301(9), shall immediately report or have a report made of such knowledge or suspicion to either the Metropolitan Police Department of the District of Columbia or the Child and Family Services Agency.
**Privileged Communications:** neither the spouse or domestic partner privilege nor the physician-patient privilege shall be grounds for excluding evidence in any proceeding in the Family Division of the Superior Court of the District of Columbia concerning the welfare of a neglected child; provided, that a judge of the Family Division of the Superior Court of the District of Columbia determines such privilege should be waived in the interest of justice.

**Procedures:** D.C. Code Ann. § §4–1321.03
**Individual Responsibility:** Each person required to make a report of a known or suspected neglected child shall:
(1) Immediately make an oral report of the case to the Child and Family Services Agency or the Metropolitan Police Department of the District of Columbia; and
(2) Make a written report of the case if requested by said Division or Police or if the abuse involves drug-related activity.
**Content of Report:** The report shall include, but need not be limited to, the following information if it is known to the person making the report:
(1) The name, age, sex, and address of the following individuals:
  (A) The child who is the subject of the report;
  (B) Each of the child's siblings and other children in the household; and
  (C) Each of the child's parents or other persons responsible for the child's care;
(2) The nature and extent of the abuse or neglect of the child and any previous abuse or neglect, if known;
(3) All other information which the person making the report believes may be helpful in establishing the cause of the abuse or neglect and the identity of the person responsible for the abuse or neglect; and
(4) If the source was required to report under this subchapter, the identity and occupation of the source, how to contact the source and a statement of the actions taken by the source concerning the child.

**Immunity:** D.C. Code Ann. § 1321.04
Any person, hospital, or institution participating in good faith in the making of a report pursuant to the reporting laws shall have immunity from civil or criminal liability that might otherwise be incurred or imposed with respect to the making of the report. Any such participant shall have the same immunity with respect to participation in any judicial proceeding involving the report. In all civil or criminal proceedings concerning the child or resulting from the report, good faith shall be presumed unless rebutted.

**Failure to Report:** D.C. Code Ann. § 1321.07
Any person required to make a report under the reporting laws who willfully fails to make such a report shall be fined not more than $300 or imprisoned for not more than 90 days, or both.

**False Reporting:**
Not specifically addressed in statute.

# FLORIDA

**Definitions:** Fla. Stat. Ann. § 39.01 (2), (12), (32), (44), (46), (52), (63) (2009)
**Abuse:** any willful or threatened act that results in any physical, mental, or sexual injury or harm that causes, or is likely to cause, significant impairment of the child's physical, mental, or emotional health.
**Child or Youth:** any unmarried person under the age of 18 years who is not emancipated by order of the court and who has been alleged or found to be dependent.
**Mental Injury:** an injury to the intellectual or psychological capacity of a child as evidenced by a discernible and substantial impairment in the ability to function within the normal range.
**Neglect:** occurs when the parent, legal custodian, or caregiver deprives a child of, or allows a child to be deprived of, necessary food, clothing, shelter, or medical treatment or permits a child to live in an environment that causes significant impairment to or endangers a child's physical, mental, or emotional health.
**Physical Injury:** death, permanent or temporary disfigurement, or impairment of any body part.
**Sexual Abuse:** any penetration, however slight, of vagina/anal opening by penis; any sexual contact between genitals or anus with mouth or tongue of another person or any intrusion, including any object (not including medical purposes); any intentional touching of genitals or intimate parts; masturbation/exposure in presence of child; any form of sexual exploitation.

**Reporting:** Fla. Stat. Ann. § 39.201 (1) (2009); § 39.204 (2008)
**Who Must Report:** physicians, osteopaths, medical examiners, chiropractors, nurses, hospital personnel engaged in the admission, examination, care, or treatment of persons, other health or mental health professional; school teachers or other school officials or personnel, social workers, daycare center workers, other professional child care, foster care, residential, or institutional workers; practitioners who rely solely on spiritual means for healing, law enforcement officers; any persons.
**Circumstances:** when they know, or have reasonable cause to suspect, that a child is an abused, abandoned, or neglected child. When any person required to report or investigate cases of suspected child abuse or neglect has reasonable cause to suspect that a child died as a result of child abuse or neglect.
**Privileged Communications:** the privileged quality of communications between a husband and wife and between any professional person and his or her patient or client, and any other privileged communications except that between attorney and client, as such communication relates both to the competency of the witness and to the exclusion of confidential communications, shall not apply to communication involving the alleged perpetrator in any situation involving known or suspected child abuse or neglect and shall not constitute grounds for failure to report as required by law.

**Procedures:** Fla. Stat. Ann. § 39.201 (2)(a)-(c), (5) (2009)
**Individual Responsibility:** Each report of known or suspected child abuse, abandonment, or neglect shall be made immediately to the department's central abuse hotline on the single statewide toll-free telephone number, and if the report is of an instance of known or suspected child abuse by a non-caretaker, the call shall be immediately electronically transferred to the appropriate county sheriff's office by the central abuse hotline. If the report is an instance of known or suspected child abuse involving impregnation of a child under 16 years of age by a person 21 years of age or older, the report shall be made immediately to the appropriate county sheriff's office or other appropriate law enforcement agency.

Mandatory reporters are required to provide their names to the hotline staff. The names of reporters shall be entered into the record of the report, but shall be held confidential.

**Immunity:** Fla. Stat. Ann. § 39.203 (1) (2008)
Any person, official, or institution participating in good faith in any act authorized or required by the reporting laws, or reporting in good faith any instance of child abuse, abandonment, or neglect to any law enforcement agency, shall be immune from any civil or criminal liability which might otherwise result by reason of such action.

Except as provided by this chapter, nothing contained in this section shall be deemed to grant immunity, civil or criminal, to any person suspected of having abused, abandoned, or neglected a child or committed any illegal act upon or against a child.

**Failure to Report:** Fla. Stat. Ann. § 39.205 (1) (2008)
A person who is required by law to report known or suspected child abuse, abandonment, or neglect and who knowingly and willfully fails to do so, or who knowingly and willfully prevents another person from doing so, is guilty of a misdemeanor of the first degree.

**False Reporting:** Fla. Stat. Ann. § 39.205 (6) (2008); § 39.206 (1) (2008)
A person who knowingly and willfully makes a false report of child abuse, abandonment, or neglect, or who advises another to make a false report, is guilty of a felony of the third degree, punishable as provided by law.

In addition to any other penalty authorized by law, the Department may impose a fine, not to exceed $10,000 for each violation, upon a person who knowingly and willfully makes a false report of abuse, abandonment, or neglect of a child, or a person who counsels another to make a false report.

# GEORGIA

**Definitions:** Ga. Code Ann. § 19-7-5 (b) (2009)
**Abused:** subjected to child abuse.
**Child:** any person under 18 years of age.
**Child Abuse:** physical injury or death inflicted upon a child by a parent or caretaker thereof by other than accidental means; however, physical forms of discipline may be used as long as there is no physical injury; neglect or exploitation of a child by a parent or caretaker; sexual abuse of a child; or sexual exploitation.
**Sexual Abuse:** a person's employing, using, persuading, enticing, or coercing any minor who is not that person's spouse to engage in sexual intercourse (genital-genital, oral-genital, anal-genital, oral-anal—persons of same or opposite sex); bestiality; masturbation; lewd exhibition of genital or pubic area; flagellation or torture by or upon a person who is nude; condition of being bound or restrained by a nude person; physical contact for sexual stimulation of genitals, pubic area, buttocks, or female breasts whether clothed or unclothed; defecation or urination for sexual stimulation; penetration of vagina or rectum by any object not part of a recognized medical procedure.
**Sexual Exploitation:** conduct by a child's parent or caretaker who allows, encourages, or requires child engagement in prostitution, or sexually explicit conduct for producing visual or print media of such conduct.

**Reporting:** GA. CODE ANN. § 19-7-5 (c), (g) (2009)
**Who Must Report:** physicians licensed to practice medicine; interns; residents; hospital/medical personnel; dentists; podiatrists; registered professional nurses/licensed practical nurses; school teachers, administrators, and guidance counselors; visiting teachers; school social workers or psychologists; licensed psychologists; interns obtaining licensing as psychologists; professional counselors; social workers, and marriage/family therapists; child-counseling personnel; child welfare agency personnel; child service organization personnel; law enforcement personnel; persons who process or produce visual or printed matter.
**Circumstances:** when they have reasonable cause to believe that a child has been abused.
**Privileged Communications:** mandatory reporters are required to report even if the reasonable cause to believe such abuse has occurred or is occurring is based in whole or in part on any communication to the reporter which would otherwise be privileged or confidential, by law.

**Procedures:** GA. CODE ANN. § 19-7-5 (c)(2), (d), (e) (2008)
**Individual Responsibility:** if a person is required to report abuse pursuant to the reporting laws because that person attends to a child pursuant to such person's duties as a member of the staff of a hospital, school, social agency, or similar facility, that person shall notify the person in charge of the facility or the designated delegate. The person so notified shall report or cause a report to be made. A staff member who makes a report to the person designated pursuant to this paragraph shall be deemed to have fully complied with this subsection. An oral report shall be made within 24 hours by telephone or otherwise and followed by a report in writing, if requested, to a child welfare agency providing services, as designate by the Department of Human Resources, or to an appropriate police authority or district attorney.
**Content of Report:** reports shall contain the names and addresses of the child and the child's parents or caretakers, if known, the child's age, the nature and extent of the child's injuries, including any evidence of previous injuries, and any other information that the reporting person believes might be helpful in establishing the cause of the injuries and the identity of the perpetrator. Photographs of injuries may be taken without the permission of the child's parent or guardian; provided that photographs do not reveal the subject's identity and are made available as soon as possible to the welfare agency providing services and to police authority.

**Immunity:** GA. CODE ANN. § 19-7-5 (f) (2009)
Any person(s), partnership, firm, corporation, association, hospital, or other entity participating in the making of a report or causing a report to be made to a child welfare agency providing protective services or to an appropriate police authority pursuant to the reporting laws or any other law, or participating in any judicial proceeding or any other proceeding resulting there from shall in so doing be immune from any civil or criminal liability that might otherwise be incurred or imposed; provided such participation is made in good faith. Any person making a report, whether required by reporting laws or not, shall be immune from liability.

**Failure to Report:** GA. CODE ANN. § 19-7-5 (h) (2000)
Any person or official required by law to report a suspected case of child abuse who knowingly and willfully fails to do so shall be guilty of a misdemeanor.

**False Reporting:**
Not specifically addressed in statute.

# HAWAII

**Definitions:** Haw. Rev. Stat. § 350–1 (2008)
**Child Abuse or Neglect:** acts or omissions of any person, or a legal entity which, is in any manner or degree related to the child, is residing with the child, or is otherwise responsible for the child's care that have resulted in the physical or psychological health or welfare of the child, who is under the age of 18, to be harmed, or to be subject to any reasonably foreseeable, substantial risk of being harmed. The acts or omissions are indicated by circumstances that include, but are not limited to, evidence of substantial/multiple skin bruising or internal bleeding; any injury causing substantial bleeding; malnutrition; failure to thrive; burns; poisoning; fractures of bone; subdural hematoma; soft tissue swelling; extreme pain; mental distress; gross degradation; death; and such injury that is not justifiably explained or at variance with conditions or circumstances; sexual contact or conduct, including, but not limited to, sexual assault as defined in the Penal Code, molestation, sexual fondling, incest, or prostitution; obscene or pornographic photographing; or other forms of sexual exploitation; or when there is injury to the psychological capacity, evidenced by substantial impairment in the child's ability to function; or when the child is not provided adequate food, clothing, shelter, psychological/physical/medical care and supervision; or when the child is provided with dangerous/harmful/detrimental drugs; this paragraph shall not apply when such drugs are provided by direction or prescription of a practitioner.

**Reporting:** Haw. Rev. Stat. § 350–1.1 (a) (1998); § 350–5 (2008)
**Who Must Report:** licensed or registered professionals of the healing arts and health-related occupations who examine, attend, treat, or provide other professional/specialized services, including, but not limited to, physicians, physicians in training, psychologists, dentists, nurses, osteopathic physicians, surgeons, optometrists, chiropractors, podiatrists; medical examiners; coroners; employees or officers of any public or private school; individual providers of child care, any licensed or registered child care facility, foster home, or similar institution; any public or private agency or institution, or other individuals providing social, medical, hospital or mental health services, including financial assistance; any law enforcement agency, including, the courts, police departments, correctional institutions, and parole or probation offices; any public or private agency providing recreational or sports activities.
**Circumstances:** when, in their professional or official capacity, they have reason to believe that child abuse or neglect has occurred, or there exists a substantial risk that child abuse or neglect may occur in the reasonably foreseeable future.
**Privileged Communications:** the physician–patient privilege, the psychologist–client privilege, the spousal privilege, and the victim–counselor privilege shall not be grounds for excluding evidence in any judicial proceeding resulting from a report of child abuse or neglect pursuant to the law.

**Procedures:** Haw. Rev. Stat. § 350–1.1 (a)-(d) (2008)
**Individual Responsibility:** notwithstanding any other state law concerning confidentiality to the contrary, mandated reporters who, in their professional or official capacity, have reason to believe that child abuse or neglect has occurred or that there exists a substantial risk that child abuse or neglect may occur in the reasonably foreseeable future, shall immediately report the matter orally to the Department of Human Services or the police department. Whenever a person designated as a mandated reporter is a member of the staff of any public or private school, agency, or institution, that staff member shall immediately notify the person in charge, or a designated delegate, who shall immediately report, or cause reports to be made, in accordance with the reporting laws.
**Content of Report:** all written reports shall contain, if known, the name and address of the child and the child's parents or other person responsible for the child's care; the child's age; the nature and extent of the child's injuries; and any other information that the reporter believes might be helpful or relevant to the investigation of the child abuse or neglect.

**Immunity:** Haw. Rev. Stat. § 350–3 (2008)
Anyone participation in good faith in the making of a report pursuant to the reporting laws shall have immunity from any civil or criminal liability that might otherwise be incurred or imposed by or as a result of making the report. Any such participant shall have the same immunity with respect to participation in any judicial proceeding resulting from such report.
Upon receiving a report, any individual within the Department of Human Services who assumes a duty or responsibility pursuant to statute shall have immunity from civil liability for acts or omissions performed within the scope of the individual's duty or responsibility.

**Failure to Report:** Haw. Rev. Stat. § 350-1.2 (2008)
Any mandatory reporter who knowingly prevents another person from reporting or who knowingly fails to provide information as required by the reporting laws shall be guilty of a petty misdemeanor.

**False Reporting:**
Not specifically addressed in statute.

# IDAHO

**Definitions:** Idaho Code § 16-1602 (1), (2), (24), (25) (2008)
**Abused:** any case in which a child is victim of (1) conduct/omission resulting in skin bruising, bleeding, malnutrition, burns, fractures, subdural hematoma, soft tissue swelling, failure to thrive, or death, and such condition or death is not justifiably explained, or where the history is at variance with the degree or type of such condition or death, or the circumstances indicate that such condition may not be the product of accidental occurrence; or (2) sexual conduct including rape, molestation, incest, prostitution, obscene or pornographic photographing, filming, or depiction for commercial purposes, or other similar forms of sexual exploitation harming/threatening the child's health or welfare or mental injury to the child.
**Abandoned:** failure of parent to maintain a parental relationship with child, including, but not limited to, reasonable support or regular personal contact.
**Mental Injury:** a substantial impairment in intellectual or psychological ability to function w/in a normal range of behavior for any period of time.
**Neglected:** a child who is w/o proper parental care/control, subsistence, education, medical or other care necessary for well-being because of the conduct or omission of parent/guardian or neglect or refusal to provide; or whose parents are unable because of incarceration, hospitalization, or other physical or mental incapacity; or who has been placed for care/adoption illegally.

**Reporting:** Idaho Code § 16-1605 (1), (3) (2008)
**Who Must Report:** physicians; residents on hospital staffs; interns; nurses; coroners; school teachers; daycare personnel; social workers; and any other person.
**Circumstances:** when they have reason to believe that a child under the age of 18 has been abused, abandoned, or neglected; when they observe a child being subjected to conditions or circumstances that would reasonably result in abuse, abandonment, or neglect.
**Privileged Communications:** Notification requirements do not apply to a duly ordained minister of religion, with regard to any confession or confidential communication made to him in his ecclesiastical capacity in the course of discipline enjoined by the church if the church is tax exempt under federal statute, confession or communication was made directly to the minister, and the confession or communication was made in the manner and context that places the minister under a level of confidentiality considered inviolate by canon law or church doctrine.
Any privilege between husband and wife or between any professional person except the lawyer-client privilege, including but not limited to physicians, counselors, hospitals, clinics, day care centers and schools and their clients, shall not be grounds for excluding evidence at any proceeding regarding the abuse, abandonment, or neglect of the child or the cause thereof.

**Procedures:** Idaho Code § 16-1605(1) (2008)
**Individual Responsibility:** Any mandated reporter having reason to believe that a child under the age of 18 years has been abused, abandoned, or neglected or who observes the child being subjected to conditions or circumstances which would reasonably result in abuse, abandonment, or neglect shall report or cause to be reported within 24 hours of such conditions or circumstances to the proper law enforcement agency or the Department of Health and Welfare.
When the attendance of a physician, resident, intern, nurse, day care worker, or social worker is pursuant to the performance of services as a member of the staff of a hospital or similar institution, he shall notify the person in charge of the institution or his designated delegate who shall make the necessary reports.

**Immunity:** IDAHO CODE § 16-1606 (2008)
Any person who has reason to believe that a child has been abused, abandoned, or neglected and, acting upon that belief, makes a report as required by the reporting laws shall have immunity from any civil or criminal liability that might otherwise be incurred or imposed. Any such participant shall have the same immunity with respect to participation in any judicial proceeding resulting from such report.
Any person who reports in bad faith or with malice shall not be protected by this law.

**Failure to Report:** IDAHO CODE § 16-1605 (4) (2008)
Failure to report as required by the reporting laws shall be a misdemeanor.

**False Reporting:** IDAHO CODE § 16-1607(2008)
Any person who makes a report or allegation of child abuse, abandonment, or neglect knowing the information to be false or who reports or alleges the same in bad faith or with malice shall be liable to the party or parties against whom the report was made for the amount of actual damages sustained or statutory damages of $2,500, whichever is greater, plus attorney's fees and costs of suit.

# ILLINOIS

**Definitions:** 325 ILL. COMP. STAT. ANN. 5/3 (2008)
**Child:** any person under the age of 18 years, unless emancipated by reason of marriage or entry into the U. S. armed services.
**Abused Child:** a child whose parent or immediate family, or any person responsible for the child's welfare, or any individual residing in the home, or a paramour of the child's parent inflicts, causes or allows physical injury, or a substantial risk of injury, by other than accidental means, which causes death, disfigurement, impairment of physical or emotional health, or loss or impairment of any body function of child; commits or allows a sex offense against such child, defined in Criminal Code of 1961 (amended), extending definitions to children under 18; commits or allows an act of torture; inflicts excessive corporal punishment; commits or allows female genital mutilation.
**Neglected Child:** any child who is not receiving the necessary nourishment or medically indicated treatment including food or care not provided solely on the basis of the present/anticipated mental or physical impairment determined by a physician(s) or otherwise is not receiving the proper support or medical/remedial care recognized under state law, including adequate food, clothing, and shelter; or who is abandoned by parents or other custodian w/o a proper plan of care; or who is a newborn whose blood, urine, or meconium has any controlled substance or metabolite defined by the Controlled Substances Act.

**Reporting:** 325 ILL. COMP. STAT. ANN. 5/4 (2008); 720 ILL. COMP. STAT. ANN. 5/11-20.2 (2008)
**Who Must Report:** physicians, residents, interns, hospital administrators engaged in examination/care/treatment, surgeons, physician assistants, dentists, hygienists, osteopaths, chiropractors, podiatrists, coroners, medical examiners, E.M.T.s, registered or licensed practical nurses, acupuncturists; school personnel, educational advocates assigned to child pursuant to law, directors/staff assistants of nursery or child care centers, recreational/facility personnel, child care workers, homemakers; substance abuse treatment personnel, crisis/hotline personnel, social workers, domestic violence personnel, registered psychologists and directly supervised assistants, psychiatrists, Christian Science practitioners; social services and general assistance administrators, foster parents, personnel of the Dep't of Public Aid, Public Health, Mental Health, Corrections, Human Rights, Rehabilitation Services, or Children and Family Services; truant, law and probation officers, funeral home employees; film/photographic processors.
**Circumstances:** when they have reasonable cause to believe a child known to them in their professional/official capacity may be an abused or neglected child.
**Privileged Communications:** The privileged communication b/t any professional person required to report and patient/client shall not apply to situations of child abuse or neglect and shall not constitute grounds for failure to report.

**Procedures:** 325 Ill. Comp. Stat. Ann. 5/4, 5/7 (2009)
**Individual Responsibility:** Any mandated reporter having reasonable cause to believe a child known to them in their professional or official capacity may be an abused child or a neglected child shall immediately report or cause a report to be made to the Department of Children and Family Services.

When in the capacity of a member of staff, the person may also notify the person in charge of such institution, school, facility or agency. Under no circumstances shall any person in charge of such institution exercise any control, modification, or other change in the report or the forwarding of such report to the Department.

All reports made under the reporting laws shall be made immediately by telephone to the central register on the single, statewide, tool-free telephone number, or in person or by telephone through the nearest Department office. All reports by mandated reporters shall be confirmed in writing to the appropriate CPS Unit, on forms supplied by the Department within 48 hours of initial report.

**Content of Report:** The report shall include, if known, the name and address of the child and his parents or custodians; the child's age; the nature of the child's condition, including any evidence of previous injuries/disabilities; and any other information that the person filing the report believes might be helpful in establishing the cause or identity of the suspected perpetrator.

**Immunity:** 325 Ill. Comp. Stat. Ann. 5/9 (2008)
Any person, institution, or agency, under the reporting laws, participating in good faith in the making of a report or referral, or in the investigation of such a report or referral, or in the taking of photographs and x-rays, or in the retaining a child in temporary protective custody, or in making a disclosure of information concerning reports of child abuse and neglect in compliance with the reporting laws, shall have immunity from any civil, criminal, or other liability that might result by reason of such actions.

For the purpose of any civil or criminal proceedings, the good faith of any persons required or permitted to report or refer under the reporting laws, or required to disclose information concerning reports of child abuse and neglect, shall be presumed.

**Failure to Report:** 325 Ill. Comp. Stat. Ann. 5/4, 5/4.02 (2008)
Any person who knowingly and willfully violates any provision of this Section other than a second or subsequent violation of transmitting a false report shall be guilty of a Class A misdemeanor.

Any physician who willfully fails to report suspected child abuse or neglect as required by this Act shall be referred to the Illinois State Medical Disciplinary Board for action in accordance with the Medical Practice Act of 1987. Any other person required by this Act to report suspected child abuse and neglect who willfully fails to report such shall be guilty of a Class A misdemeanor.

**False Reporting:** 325 Ill. Comp. Stat. Ann. 5/4 (2008)
Any person who knowingly transmits a false report to the Department of Children and Family Services commits the offense of disorderly conduct under the law. Any person who violates this provision a second or subsequent time shall be guilty of a Class 4 felony.

# INDIANA

**Definitions:** Ind. Code Ann. § 31-9-2-14 (a) (2008); § 31-34-7-4 (2008)
**Child in Need of Services:** if before the child becomes 18 years of age: the child's physical or mental condition is seriously impaired/endangered as a result of inability, refusal, or neglect of the child's parent/guardian to supply the child w/necessary food, clothing, shelter, medical care, education, or supervision; the child is the victim of a sex offense as defined in criminal statutes (Ind. Code Ann. § 35-42-4); the child's parent or guardian allows the child to participate in an obscene performance or commit a sex offense as defined by criminal statutes; the child substantially endangers the child's own health or health of another individual; the child's parent or guardian fails to participate in a disciplinary proceeding in connection with the student's improper behavior, if the behavior of the student has been repeatedly disruptive in the school; the child is a missing child; and the child needs care (including care for fetal alcohol syndrome or born with any amount of a controlled substance that causes abnormal, threatening injuries) that the child is not receiving; and is unlikely to be provided or accepted without the coercive intervention of the court.

This includes deprivation of medical intervention necessary to remedy a life-threatening condition, generally provided to similarly situated children w/or w/o disabilities.

**Reporting:** IND. CODE ANN. § 31-33-5 (1)-(2); § 31-33-6-2 (2008)
**Who Must Report:** any individual; any staff member of a medical or other public or private institution, school, facility, or agency.
**Circumstances:** when they have reason to believe that a child is a victim of child abuse or neglect.
**Privileged Communications:** The following privileged communications are not grounds for failing to report as required by the reporting laws: between a husband and wife; between a health care provider and that health care provider's patient; between a certified social worker, certified clinical social workers, or certified marriage and family therapist and a client of any of these professionals; or between a school counselor or psychologist and a student.

**Procedures:** IND. CODE ANN. § 31-33-5 (1)-(4) (2008)
**Individual Responsibility:** A person who has a duty to report under the reporting law that a child may be a victim of child abuse or neglect shall immediately make an oral report to the local child protection service, or to the local law enforcement agency.
 If an individual is required to make a report under the reporting law in the individual's capacity as a member of the staff of a medical or other public or private institution, school, facility, or agency, the individual shall immediately notify the individual in charge of the institution, school, facility or agency or the designated agent of the individual in charge.
 The individual so notified shall report or cause a report to be made.
 This provision does not relieve an individual of the obligation to report on his or her behalf, unless a report has already been made to the best of the individual's belief.

**Immunity:** IND. CODE ANN. § 31-33-6 (1)-(3) (2007)
 A person, other than a person accused of child abuse or neglect, who makes or causes to be made a report of a child who may be a victim of child abuse or neglect; is a health care provider and detains a child for purposes of causing photographs, x-rays, or a physical medical examination to be made; makes any other report of a child who may be a victim of child abuse or neglect, or participates in any judicial proceeding or other proceeding resulting from a report that a child may be a victim of child abuse or neglect; or relating to the subject matter of the report; is immune from any civil or criminal liability that might otherwise be imposed because of such actions.
 Immunity does not attach to such action for a person who has acted maliciously or in bad faith.
 A person making a report that a child may be a victim of child abuse or neglect or assisting in any requirement of the reporting laws is presumed to have acted in good faith.

**Failure to Report:** IND. CODE ANN. § 31-33-22-1 (2008)
 A person who knowingly fails to make a report required by law commits a Class B misdemeanor.
 A person who in his capacity as a staff member of a medical or other institution, school, facility, or agency is required to make a report to the individual in charge of the institution, school, facility, or agency or his designated agent, and who knowingly fails to make a report commits a Class B misdemeanor. This penalty is imposed in addition to the penalty imposed in subsection (a).

**False Reporting:** IND. CODE ANN. § 31-33-22-3 (a)-(b) (2007)
 A person who intentionally communicates to a law enforcement agency or a local child protection service a report of child abuse or neglect knowing the report to be false commits a Class A misdemeanor. However, the offense is a Class D felony if the person has a previous unrelated conviction for making a report of child abuse or neglect knowing the report to be false.
 A person who intentionally communicates to a law enforcement agency or a local child protection service a report of child abuse or neglect knowing the report to be false is liable to the person accused of child abuse or neglect for actual damages. The finder of fact may award punitive damages and attorney's fees in an amount determined by the finder of fact against the person.

# IOWA

**Definitions:** IOWA CODE ANN. § 232.68 (2) (2008)
**Child Abuse or Neglect:** any non-accidental physical injury, or injury which is at variance with the history given of it, suffered by a child as a result of acts/omissions of a person responsible for the child; any mental injury to a child's intellectual or psychological capacity as evidenced by an observable and substantial impairment in the child's ability to function w/in the normal range of performance and behavior as the result of the acts/omissions of a person responsible for the child, if the impairment is diagnosed and confirmed by a licensed physician or qualified mental health professional; the commission of a sexual offense with or to a child, pursuant to law relating to sexual offenses on children, as a result of the acts/omissions of the person responsible for the child, the commission of which includes any sexual offense with or to a person under age 18, unless the law states otherwise; the failure on the part of a person responsible for a child to provide the adequate food, shelter, clothing, or other care necessary for the child's health and welfare when financially able to do so or when offered financial or other reasonable means to do so; the acts/omissions of a person responsible for a child that allow, permit, or encourage the child to engage in prostitution with or to a person under age 18, unless the law states otherwise; or an illegal drug is present in a child's body as a direct and foreseeable consequence of the acts/omissions of the person responsible for the child.

**Reporting:** IOWA CODE ANN. § 232.69 (1)(a)-(b) (2008)
**Who Must Report:** self-employed social workers; social workers under the jurisdiction of the Dept. of Human Services or employed by a public/private agency, certified psychologists; licensed school employees; employees or operators of public or private health care facilities, licensed child care center, registered group day care home, registered family day care home, substance abuse programs or facilities, juvenile detention or shelter care facilities, which is approved as such, foster care facilities, licensed or approved as such, or mental health centers; employees of Dept. of Human Services; peace officers, dental hygienists, counselors, mental health professional (IOWA CODE ANN. § 232.68 (7)); commercial film/photographic print processors.
**Circumstances:** mandated reporters shall make a report of abuse of a child who is under 12 years of age and may make a report of abuse of a child who is 12 years of age or older, which would be defined as child abuse under the definition of abuse referring to sexual crimes, except that the abuse resulted from the acts/omissions of a person other than a person responsible for the child. Every health practitioner who in the scope of professional practice examines/treats a child and reasonably believes the child has been abused or has suffered abuse is required to report, including a health practitioner who receives information confirming that a child is infected w/a sexually transmitted disease, unless law requires otherwise.

**Procedures:** IOWA CODE ANN. § 232.69 (1) (2008); § 232.70 (1)-(7) (2008)
**Individual Responsibility:** A person mandated to report shall make a report within 24 hours. Each report made by a mandatory reporter shall be made both orally and in writing. The oral report shall be made by telephone or otherwise to the Dept. of Human Services. If the person making the report has reason to believe that immediate protection for the child is advisable, that person shall also make an oral report to an appropriate law enforcement agency. The written report shall be made to the Dept. of Human Services within 48 hours after such oral report.
**Content of Report:** oral and written reports shall contain the following, or as much thereof as the person making the report is able to furnish: names and home address of the child and the child's parents or persons believed to be responsible for the child; child's present location if not the same as the parents or person responsible for the child; child's age; nature and extent of child's injuries, including any evidence of previous injuries; name, age, and condition of other children in the same house; any other information that the person making the report believes might be helpful in establishing the cause of the injury to the child, the identity of the person or persons responsible for the injury, or in providing assistance to the child; and the name and address of the person making the report.

**Immunity:** Iowa Code Ann. § 232.74 (2008)
A person participating in good faith in the making of a report, photographs, or x-rays, or in the performance of a medically relevant test pursuant to the reporting laws or aiding and assisting in an investigation of a child abuse report pursuant to the reporting laws shall have immunity from any civil or criminal liability which might otherwise be incurred or imposed. The person shall have the same immunity with respect to participation in good faith in any judicial proceeding resulting from the report or relating to the subject matter of the report.

**Failure to Report:** Iowa Code Ann. § 232.75 (1)-(2) (2007)
Any person, official, agency, or institution required by law to report a suspected case of child abuse who knowingly and willfully fails to do so is guilty of a simple misdemeanor; and who knowingly fails to do so is civilly liable for the damages proximately caused by such failure.

**False Reporting:** Iowa Code Ann. § 232.75 (3) (2007)
A person who reports or causes to be reported to the Department false information regarding an alleged act of child abuse, knowing that the information is false or that the act did not occur, commits a simple misdemeanor.

# KANSAS

**Definitions:** Kan. Stat. Ann. § 38-2202 (d), (s), (cc) (2006)
**Child in Need of Care:** a person less than 18 years of age who is without adequate parental care, control or subsistence and the condition is not due solely to the lack of financial means of the child's parents or custodian; is without the care or control necessary for the child's physical, mental, or emotional health; has been physically, mentally, or emotionally abused or neglected or sexually abused; has been placed for care or adoption in violation of law; has been abandoned or does not have a known living parent; is not attending school as required by state law; has been residing in the same residence with a sibling or another person under 18 years of age who has been physically, mentally, or emotionally abused or neglected, or sexually abused.
**Physical, Mental or Emotional Abuse or Neglect:** the infliction of physical, mental or emotional injury or the causing of a deterioration of a child and may include, but not limited to, failing to maintain reasonable care, negligent or maltreatment or exploiting a child to the extent that the child' health or emotional well-being is endangered; failure to use resources available to treat a diagnosed medical condition if such treatment will make a child substantially more comfortable, reduce pain and suffering, or correct or substantially diminish a crippling condition from worsening.
**Sexual Abuse:** means any contact or interaction with a child in which the child is being used for the sexual stimulation of the perpetrator, the child or another person. Sexual abuse shall include allowing, permitting or encouraging a child to engage in prostitution or to be photographed, filmed or depicted in pornographic material.

**Reporting:** Kan. Stat. Ann. § 38-2223 (2006)
**Who Must Report:** persons licensed to practice the healing arts or dentistry; persons licensed to practice optometry; persons engaged in post graduate training programs approved by the State Board of Healing Arts; licensed professional or practical nurses examining, attending, or treating a child under the age of 18; chief administrative officers of medical care facilities; emergency medical service personnel; teachers, school administrators, or other employees of a school which the child is attending; person licensed by the Secretary of Health and Environment to provide child care services or the employees of persons so licensed at the place where the child care services are being provided to the child; licensed psychologists; registering marriage and family therapists; licensed social workers; firefighters; mediators appointed under the law; law enforcement officers; juvenile intake and assessment workers.
**Circumstances:** when they have reason to suspect that a child has been injured as a result of physical, mental, or emotional abuse or neglect, or sexual abuse; when they know of the death of a child.

**Procedures:** Kan. Stat. Ann. § 38-2223(a)-(c) (2006)
**Individual Responsibility:** when any mandated reporter or other person has reason to suspect that a child has been injured as a result of physical, mental or emotional abuse, or neglect or sexual abuse, the person shall report the matter promptly. The report may be made orally and shall be followed by a written report if requested. When the suspicion results from a medical examination or treatment of a child in a facility or similar institution, the staff member shall immediately notify the manager or person in charge who shall make a written report. Reports shall be made to the state Dept. of Social and Rehabilitative Services; and when not open, to the appropriate law enforcement agency. Reports from an institution operated by the Secr. of Social and Rehabilitation Services or the commissioner of juvenile justice shall be made to the Attorney General. All others by persons employed by or of children of employees of the state Dept. of Social and Rehabilitation Services or juvenile justice shall be made to the appropriate law enforcement agency.
**Content of Report:** every written report shall contain, if known, the names and addresses of the child and the child's parents or persons responsible for the child's care, the child's age, the nature and extent of the child's injury (including any evidence of previous injuries) and any other information that the reporter believes might be helpful in establishing the cause of the injuries and the identity of the persons responsible for them.

**Immunity:** Kan. Stat. Ann. § 38-2223(f) (2006)
Anyone participating without malice in the making of an oral or written report to a law enforcement agency or to the Dept. of Social and Rehabilitation Services relating to injuries inflicted upon a child as a result of physical, mental, sexual, or emotional abuse or neglect, or in any follow-up activity to or investigation of the report shall have immunity from any civil liability that might otherwise be incurred or imposed. Any such participant shall have the same immunity with respect to participation in any judicial proceedings resulting form the report.

**Failure to Report:** Kan. Stat. Ann. § 38-2223 (e) (2006)
Willful and knowing failure to make a report required by the reporting laws is a Class B misdemeanor.
Preventing, or interfering with the intent to prevent, the making of a report required by the reporting laws is a Class B misdemeanor.

**False Reporting:** Kan. Stat. Ann. § 38-2223 (e) (2006)
Any person who willfully and knowingly makes a false report pursuant to this section or makes a report that such person knows lacks factual foundation is guilty of a class B misdemeanor.

# KENTUCKY

**Definitions:** Ky. Rev. Stat. Ann. § 600.020 (1), (55), (2007)
**Abused or Neglected Child:** a child whose health or welfare is harmed or threatened with harm when his or her parent, guardian, or other person exercising custodial control or supervision of the child: inflicts or allows to be inflicted upon the child physical or emotional injury as defined below by other than accidental means; creates or allows to be created a risk of physical or emotional injury to the child by other than accidental means; engages in a pattern of conduct that renders the parent incapable of caring for the immediate and ongoing needs of the child, including but not limited to, parental incapacity due to alcohol and other drug use; continuously or repeatedly fails or refuses to provide essential parental care and protection for the child, considering the age of the child; commits or allows to be committed an act of sexual abuse, sexual exploitation, or prostitution upon the child; creates or allows to be created a risk that an act of sexual abuse, sexual exploitation, or prostitution will be committed upon the child; abandons or exploits the child; does not provide the child with adequate care, supervision, food, clothing, shelter, and education or medical care necessary for the child's well-being.

**Reporting:** Ky. Rev. Stat. Ann. § 620.030 (1), (2) (2008)
**Who Must Report:** physicians, osteopathic physicians, nurses, coroners, medical examiners, residents, interns, chiropractors, dentists, optometrists, emergency medical technicians, paramedics, health professionals; teachers, school personnel, child-caring personnel; social workers, mental health professionals, peace officers; any organization or agency for any of the above persons; any persons.
**Circumstances:** when they know or have reasonable cause to believe that a child is dependent, neglected, or abused.
**Privileged Communications:** neither the husband–wife nor any professional–client/patient privilege, except the attorney–client and clergy–penitent privilege, shall be a ground for refusing to report, or for excluding evidence regarding a dependent, neglected, or abuse child thereof, in any judicial proceedings resulting from a report.

**Procedures:** Ky. Rev. Stat. Ann. § 620.030 (2008)
**Individual Responsibility:** any person who knows or has reasonable cause to believe that a child is dependent, neglected, or abused shall immediately cause an oral or written report to be made to a local law enforcement agency of the Kentucky State Police; the Cabinet for Families and Children or its designated representative; the Commonwealth's attorney or the county attorney; by telephone or otherwise. Any supervisor who receives from an employee a report of suspected dependency, neglect, or abuse shall promptly make a report to the proper authorities for investigation. Nothing in this section shall relieve individuals of their obligation to report.

Any mandated reporter shall, if requested, file a written report with the local law enforcement agency or the Kentucky State police or the Commonwealth's attorney or county attorney, the Cabinet for Families and Children or its designated representative within 48 hours of the original report.
**Content of Report:** the written report shall contain the names and addresses of the child and his parents or other custodian; the child's age; the nature/extent of the child's alleged dependency, neglect or abuse (including any previous charges) to child or his siblings; the name and address of the person allegedly responsible for the abuse or neglect; and any other information that the reporter believes may be helpful in the furtherance of the reporting laws.

**Immunity:** Ky. Rev. Stat. Ann. § 620.050 (1) (2007)
Anyone acting upon reasonable cause in the making of a report in good faith shall have immunity from any civil or criminal liability that might otherwise be incurred or imposed. Any such participant shall have the same immunity with respect to participation in any judicial proceeding resulting from such report or action.

**Failure to Report:**
Not specifically addressed in statute.

**False Reporting:** Ky. Rev. Stat. Ann. § 620.050 (1) (2008)
Any person who knowingly makes a false report and does so with malice shall be guilty of a Class A misdemeanor.

# LOUISIANA

**Definitions:** La. Children's Code Ann. art. 603 (1), (5), (7), (16) (2008)
**Abuse:** includes any one of the following acts which seriously endangers the physical, mental, or emotional health of the child: the infliction, attempted infliction, or, as a result of inadequate supervision, the allowance of the infliction or attempted infliction of physical or mental injury upon the child by a parent or any other person; the exploitation or overwork of a child by a parent or any other person; the involvement of the child in any sexual act with a parent or any other person, or the aiding or tolerance by the parent or caretaker of the child's sexual involvement with any other person or of the child's involvement in pornographic displays, or any other involvement of a child in a sexual activity constituting a crime under the laws of the state.
**Child:** a person under 18 years of age who, prior to juvenile proceedings, has not been judicially emancipated, or emancipated by marriage.
**Child Pornography:** the visual depiction of a child engaged in actual or simulated intercourse, deviate sexual intercourse, sexual bestiality, masturbation, sadomasochistic abuse, or lewd exhibition of the genitals.
**Neglect:** the refusal or willful failure of a parent or caretaker to supply the child with necessary food, clothing, shelter, care, treatment or counseling for any injury, illness, or condition, that substantially threatens or impairs the child's physical, mental, or emotional health.

**Reporting:** La. Children's Code Ann. art. 603 (13), 603 (15), 610(F) (2008); 609 (2008)
**Who Must Report:** any of the following individuals performing their occupational duties: health practitioners, including but not limited to, physicians, surgeons, physical therapists, dentists, paramedics, optometrists, coroners, or medical examiners; teachers or child care providers, including but not limited to, school principals, teacher's aides, foster home parents, or group home staff members; mental health/social service practitioners, including but not limited to, psychiatrists, psychologists, marriage and family counselors, and social workers; police officers, law enforcement officials; commercial film or photographic print processors.
**Circumstances:** when they have cause to believe that a child's physical or mental health or welfare is endangered as a result of abuse or neglect, or abuse or neglect was a contributing factor in a child's death.
**Privileged Communications:** when a priest, rabbi, duly ordained minister, or Christian Science practitioner has acquired knowledge of abuse or neglect from a person during a confession or other sacred communication, he shall encourage that person to report but shall not be a mandatory reporter of that information given in confession or sacred communication. Notwithstanding any claim of privileged communication, any mandatory reporter shall report in accordance with the reporting laws.

**Procedures:** La. Children's Code Ann. art. 610 (2008)
**Individual Responsibility:** reports of child abuse or neglect, where the abuser is believed to be a parent or caretaker, shall be made immediately to the child protection unit of the Dept. of Social Services. Reports in which the abuse or neglect is believed to be perpetrated by someone other than a caretaker and the caretaker is not believed to have any responsibility for the abuse or neglect, shall be made immediately to a local or state law enforcement agency. If the initial report was in oral form by a mandatory reporter, it shall be followed by a written report w/in five days to the child protection unit of the Dept. of Social Services or, if necessary, to the local law enforcement agency.
**Content of Report:** the report shall contain, if known: the name, address, age, sex, and race of the child; the nature, extent, and cause of the injuries or endangered condition, including any previous known or suspected abuse to child or child's siblings; the name and address of the child's parents or caretaker; the names and ages of all other members of the child's household; the name and address of the reporter and how the child came to his/her attention; any explanation of child's injury or condition offered by child, caretaker, or any other person; any other information believed to be important. The report shall name the alleged perpetrator, if known, and the name of such person if the child names him.

**Immunity:** La. Children's Code Ann. art. 611 (2008)
Any person who in good faith makes a report, cooperates in any investigation arising as a result of such report, or participates in judicial proceedings resulting from such report, or any caseworker who in good faith conducts an investigation, makes an investigation judgment or disposition, or releases or uses information contained in the central registry for the purpose of protecting a child, shall have immunity from civil or criminal liability that otherwise might be incurred or imposed.
This immunity shall not be extended to any alleged principal, conspirator, or accessory to an offense involving the abuse or neglect of the child; or any person who makes a report known to be false or with reckless disregard for the truth of the report.

**Failure to Report:** La. Children's Code Ann. art. 609(A)(2) (2008)
A mandatory reporter who violates the duties imposed by the law is subject to criminal prosecution.

**False Reporting:** La. Children's Code Ann. art. 609(C) (2008)
The filing of a report known to be false may subject the offender to criminal prosecution authorized by law.

# MAINE

**Definitions:** ME. REV. STAT. ANN. tit. 22, § 4002 (1), (1-A), (1-B), (6) (2008)
**Abuse or Neglect:** a threat to a child's health or welfare by physical, mental, or emotional injury or impairment, sexual abuse or exploitation, deprivation of essential needs or lack of protection from these by a person responsible for the child.
**Abandonment:** any conduct on the part of the parent showing an intent to forego parental duties or relinquish parental claims, evidenced by failure for a period of at least six months to communicate meaningfully or maintain regular visitation with the child; failure to participate in any plan or program designed to reunite the parent with child; deserting the child without affording means of identifying the child and his parent or custodian; failure to respond to notice of child protective proceedings; any other conduct indicating an intent to forego parental duties or claims.
**Aggravating Factor:** with regard to parent, the subjection of child to rape, gross sexual misconduct, sexual assault, sexual abuse, incest, aggravated assault, kidnapping, promotion of prostitution, abandonment, torture, chronic abuse, or any heinous or abhorrent treatment.
**Jeopardy to Health and Welfare:** serious abuse or neglect, evidenced by deprivation of adequate food, clothing, shelter, supervision, including health care; deprivation of adequate food, clothing, shelter, supervision or care or education when the child is at least 7 years of age and has not completed grade 6; absence of any person responsible for child.

**Reporting:** ME. REV. STAT. ANN. tit. 22, § 4011-A (1) (2008); § 4015 (2008)
**Who Must Report:** medical or osteopathic physicians, residents, interns, emergency medical persons, medical examiners, physicians' assistants, dentists, dental hygienists/assistants, chiropractors, podiatrists, registered/licensed nurses, home health aides, medical workers; teachers, guidance counselors, school officials, child care personnel; social workers, psychologists, mental health professionals; court-appointed special advocates, guardians ad litem, homemakers, law enforcement officials, state/municipal fire/code inspectors, licensing board chairs having jurisdiction; clergy members; commercial film/print processors.
**Circumstances:** when acting in a professional capacity, a reporter knows or has reasonable cause to suspect that a child has been or is likely to be abused or neglected.
**Privileged Communications:** the husband–wife and physician/psychotherapist–patient privilege are abrogated in relation to required reporting, cooperating with the dept. of guardian ad litem in an investigation, other child protective activity, or giving evidence in a child protection proceeding. Information released shall be kept confidential and may not be disclosed by the dept. except as provided by law. Statements made to licensed mental health professionals in the course of counseling, therapy, or evaluation may not be used against the client in a criminal proceeding except to rebut the client's testimony.

**Procedures:** ME. REV. STAT. ANN. tit. 22, § 4011-A (1), (1-A) (2007) § 4012 (2008)
**Individual Responsibility:** reports regarding abuse or neglect shall be made immediately by telephone to the Dept. of Human Services and shall be followed by a written report within 48 hours if requested by the Department. A member of the staff of a medical or public or private institution, agency or facility shall immediately notify the designated agent, who shall then cause a report to be made. The staff may also make a report. When abuse or neglect is by a person not responsible for child, a reporter shall immediately report or cause a report to be made to the district attorney's office.

When licensed mental health professionals are required to report, the report is to be made to the Dept. of Human Services. Agreement can be made on how the report is to be pursued regarding treatment or prosecution. This encourages offenders to seek/use treatment.
**Content of Report:** reports shall contain, if known: the name and address of the child and the persons responsible for his or her care; the child's age and sex; nature/extent of abuse/neglect; a description of injuries, sexual abuse or exploitation and any explanation given; family composition and evidence of prior abuse of child or siblings; the source and the person making the report, his or her occupation and where he or she can be contacted; the actions taken by the source; any other helpful information.

**Immunity:** ME. REV. STAT. ANN. tit. 22, § 4014 (2008)
A person, including an agent of the Department, participating in good faith in reporting under the reporting laws or participating in a related child protection investigation or proceeding, including but not limited to, a multidisciplinary team, out-of-home abuse investigating team, or other investigation or treatment team, is immune from any criminal or civil liability for the act of reporting or participating in the investigation or proceeding. Good faith does not include instances when a false report is made and the person knows the report is false.

Nothing in this law may be construed to bar criminal or civil action regarding perjury or regarding the abuse or neglect that led to a report, investigation, or proceeding.

A person participating in good faith in taking photographs or x-rays pursuant to the reporting laws is immune from civil liability for invasion of privacy that might otherwise result from these actions.

In a proceeding regarding immunity from liability, there shall be a rebuttable presumption of good faith.

### Failure to Report:
Not specifically addressed in statute.

### False Reporting:
Not specifically addressed in statute.

## MARYLAND

**Definitions:** MD. CODE ANN. FAM. LAW § 5–701 (2008)
**Abuse:** the physical or mental injury of a child by a parent or other person who has permanent or temporary care or custody or responsibility for supervision of a child, or by any household or family member, under circumstances that indicate that the child's health or welfare is harmed or at substantial risk of being harmed; or sexual abuse of a child, whether physical injuries are sustained or not.
**Child:** any individual under the age of 18 years.
**Mental Injury:** the observable, identifiable, and substantial impairment of a child's mental or psychological ability to function.
**Neglect:** the leaving of a child unattended or other failure to give proper care and attention to a child by any parent or other person who has permanent or temporary care or responsibility for supervision of the child under circumstances that indicate that the child's health or welfare is harmed or placed at substantial risk of harm, or mental injury to the child or a substantial risk of mental injury.
**Sexual Abuse:** any act that involves sexual molestation or exploitation of a child by a parent or other person who has permanent or temporary care or responsibility for supervision of a child or by any household or family member. Sexual abuse includes incest, rape, a sexual offense in any degree, sodomy, and unnatural or perverted sexual practices.

**Reporting:** MD. CODE ANN. FAM. LAW § 5–704 (a) (Supp. 1998); § 5–705 (a)(2), (a)(3) (2007)
**Who Must Report:** the following persons acting in a professional capacity: health practitioners; educators or human services workers; or police officers. Any other persons.
**Circumstances:** when they have reason to believe that a child has been subjected to abuse or neglect.
**Privileged Communications:** a person is not required to provide notice in violation of the attorney–client privilege; if the notice would disclose matter communicated in confidence by a client to the client's attorney or other information relating to the representation of the client; or in violation of any constitutional right to assistance of counsel. A minister of the gospel, clergyman, or priest of an established church of any denomination is not required to provide notice if the notice would disclose matter in relation to any communication that is protected by the clergy–penitent privilege and the communication was made to the minister, clergyman, or priest in a professional character in the course of discipline enjoined by the church to which the minister, clergyman, or priest belongs; and the minister, clergyman, or priest is bound to maintain the confidentiality of that communication under canon law, church doctrine, or practice.

**Procedures:** Md. Code Ann. Fam. Law § 5–705 (a)(1) (2007); § 5–704 (2008)
**Individual Responsibility:** Notwithstanding any other provision of law, including any privileged communications, each mandated reporter, acting in a professional capacity, who has reason to believe that a child has been subjected to abuse, shall notify the local Dept. of Social Services or the appropriate law enforcement agency; or neglect, shall notify the local department. If acting as a staff member of a hospital, public health agency, child care institution, juvenile detention center, school, or similar institution, immediately notify and give all information required to the head of the institution or the designee. An oral report, by telephone or direct communication, shall be made as soon as possible to an appropriate department or agency, followed by a written report to the local department no later than 48 hours after the contact, attention, or treatment that caused the individual to believe the child had been abused or neglected, with a copy to the local State's Attorney.
**Content of Report:** Insofar as reasonably possible, a report shall include the name, age, and home address of the child; the name and home address of the child's parent or other person who is responsible for the child; the whereabouts of the child; the nature and extent of the abuse or neglect, including information of possible previous instances of abuse or neglect; and any other information that would determine the cause and the identity of any individual responsible for the abuse or neglect.

**Immunity:** Md. Code Ann. Fam. Law § 5–708 (2007)
Any person who makes or participates in making a report of abuse or neglect or participates in an investigation or resulting judicial proceeding shall have immunity from civil liability or criminal penalty.

**Failure to Report:**
Not specifically addressed in statute.

**False Reporting:**
Not specifically addressed in statute.

# MASSACHUSETTS

**Definitions:** Mass. Gen. Laws. Ann. ch. 119, § 21 (2011);
**Child:** Person under the age of 18.
**Child in Need of Services:** A child between the ages of 6 and 17 who: (a) repeatedly runs away from the home of a parent or legal guardian; (b) repeatedly fails to obey the lawful and reasonable commands of a parent or legal guardian, thereby interfering with the parent's or legal guardian's ability to adequately care for and protect the child; (c) repeatedly fails to obey lawful and reasonable school regulations; or (d) when not otherwise excused from attendance in accordance with lawful and reasonable school regulations, willfully fails to attend school for more than 8 school days in a quarter.
**Parent:** means mother or father.

**Reporting:** MASS. GEN. LAWS. ANN ch. 119, § 21 (2011); §51A (2010) § 51B (2008)
**Who Must Report:** a person who is: (i) a physician, medical intern, hospital personnel engaged in the examination, care or treatment of persons, medical examiner, psychologist, emergency medical technician, dentist, nurse, chiropractor, podiatrist, optometrist, osteopath, allied mental health and human services professional licensed under section 165 of chapter 112, drug and alcoholism counselor, psychiatrist or clinical social worker; (ii) a public or private school teacher, educational administrator, guidance or family counselor, child care worker, person paid to care for or work with a child in any public or private facility, or home or program funded by the commonwealth or licensed under chapter 15D that provides child care or residential services to children or that provides the services of child care resource and referral agencies, voucher management agencies or family child care systems or child care food programs, licensor of the department of early education and care or school attendance officer; (iii) a probation officer, clerk-magistrate of a district court, parole officer, social worker, foster parent, firefighter, police officer; (iv) a priest, rabbi, clergy member, ordained or licensed minister, leader of any church or religious body, accredited Christian Science practitioner, person performing official duties on behalf of a church or religious body that are recognized as the duties of a priest, rabbi, clergy, ordained or licensed minister, leader of any church or religious body, accredited Christian Science practitioner, or person employed by a church or religious body to supervise, educate, coach, train or counsel a child on a regular basis; (v) in charge of a medical or other public or private institution, school or facility or that person's designated agent; or (vi) the child advocate.
**Circumstances:** when, in their professional capacities, they have reasonable cause to believe that a child is: suffering physical or emotional injury resulting from abuse, or sexual abuse, which causes harm or substantial risk of harm; suffering from neglect, including malnutrition; or determined to be dependent upon an addictive drug at birth.
**Privileged Communications:**
(j) Any privilege relating to confidential communications, established by sections 135 to 135B, inclusive, of chapter 112 or by sections 20A and 20B of chapter 233, shall not prohibit the filing of a report under this section or a care and protection petition under section 24, except that a priest, rabbi, clergy member, ordained or licensed minister, leader of a church or religious body or accredited Christian Science practitioner need not report information solely gained in a confession or similarly confidential communication in other religious faiths. Nothing in the general laws shall modify or limit the duty of a priest, rabbi, clergy member, ordained or licensed minister, leader of a church or religious body or accredited Christian Science practitioner to report suspected child abuse or neglect under this section when the priest, rabbi, clergy member, ordained or licensed minister, leader of a church or religious body or accredited Christian Science practitioner is acting in some other capacity that would otherwise make him a mandated reporter.

**Procedures:** MASS. GEN. LAWS. ANN ch. 119, § 51A (2010)
**Individual Responsibility:** any mandated reporter, in their professional capacity, shall immediately report physical, emotional, or sexual abuse or neglect to the Dept. of Social Services by oral communication and by making a written report within 48 hours after such oral communication. A member of the staff of a medical or other public or private institution, school or facility shall immediately notify the Dept. of Social Services or the person in charge of such institution or that person's designated agent, whereupon such person in charge or said agent shall then become responsible to make the report.
**Content of Report:** the required reports shall contain the names and addresses of the child and his parents or other person responsible for his care, if known; the child's age, the child's sex; the nature and extent of the child's injuries, abuse, maltreatment, or neglect, including any evidence of prior injuries; the circumstances under which the person required to report first became aware of the child's injuries; whatever action, if any, was taken to treat, shelter, or otherwise assist the child; the name of the person making such report; and any other information which the person reporting believes might be helpful in establishing the cause of the injuries, the identity of the person or persons responsible there for, and such other information required by the Dept. of Social Services.

**Immunity:** Mass. Gen. Laws. Ann ch. 119, § 51A (2010)
No person required to report shall be liable in any civil or criminal action because of such report. No other person making a report shall be liable in any civil or criminal action by reason of such report if it was made in good faith; provided, however, that such person did not perpetrate or inflict the abuse or cause the neglect. Any person making such report who in the determination of the Department or the district attorney may have perpetrated or inflicted the abuse or caused the neglect, may be liable in a civil or criminal action.

**Failure to Report:** Mass. Gen. Laws. Ann. ch. 119, § 51A (2010)
Any mandated reporter who has knowledge of child abuse or neglect that resulted in serious bodily injury to or death of a child and willfully fails to report such abuse or neglect shall be punished by a fine of up to $5,000 or imprisonment in the house of correction for not more than 2 1/2 years or by both such fine and imprisonment; and, upon a guilty finding or a continuance without a finding, the court shall notify any appropriate professional licensing authority of the mandated reporter's violation of this paragraph.

**False Reporting:** Mass. Gen. Laws. Ann ch. 119, § 51A (2010)
Whoever knowingly and willfully files a frivolous report of child abuse or neglect under this section shall be punished by: (i) a fine of not more than $2,000 for the first offense; (ii) imprisonment in a house of correction for not more than 6 months and a fine of not more than $2,000 for the second offense; and (iii) imprisonment in a house of correction for not more than 2 1/2 years and a fine of not more than $2,000 for the third and subsequent offenses.

## MICHIGAN

**Definitions:** M.C.L.A. 722.622
**Child:** a person under 18 years of age.
**Child Abuse:** harm or threatened harm to a child's health or welfare by a parent, legal guardian, or any other person responsible for the child's health or welfare, or by a teacher or teacher's aide, or member of the clergy.
**Child Neglect:** harm or threatened harm to a child's health or welfare by a parent, legal guardian, or any other person responsible for the child's health or welfare that occurs through negligent treatment, including the failure to provide adequate food, clothing, shelter, or medical care; or placing a child at an unreasonable risk to the child's health or welfare by failure to intervene to eliminate that risk when that person is able to do so and has or should have knowledge of the risk.
**Sexual Abuse:** engaging in sexual contact or sexual penetration, as defined by the Michigan penal code, with a child.
**Sexual Exploitation:** includes allowing, permitting, or encouraging a child to engage in prostitution, or allowing, permitting, encouraging, or engaging in the photographing, filming, or depicting of a child engaged in a list of sexual acts as defined by the Michigan Compiled Laws.

**Reporting:** M.C.L.A. 722.623, 722.631
**Who Must Report:** physicians, coroners, dentists, registered dental hygienists, medical examiners, nurses, person licensed to provide emergency medical care, audiologists; school administrators, school counselors, school teachers, regulated child care providers; psychologists, marriage and family therapists, licensed professional counselors, certified social workers, social workers, social work technicians; law enforcement officers.
**Circumstances:** when they have reasonable cause to suspect child abuse or neglect. The pregnancy of a child less than 12 years of age or the presence of a venereal disease in a child who is over 1 month of age but less than 12 years of age shall be reasonable cause to suspect child abuse and neglect have occurred.
**Privileged Communications:** any legally recognized privileged communication, except that between attorney and client and to a member of the clergy in his/her professional character in a confession or similar confidential communication, is abrogated and shall neither constitute grounds for excusing a report otherwise required to be made or for excluding evidence in a civil child protective proceeding resulting from a report.

**Procedures:** M.C.L.A. 722.623
**Individual Responsibility:** a mandated reporter who has reasonable cause to suspect child abuse or neglect shall make immediately, by telephone or otherwise, an oral report, or cause an oral report to be made, of the suspected child abuse or neglect to the Department. Within 72 hours of making the oral report, the person shall file a written report as required in this act.

If the reporting person is a member of the staff of a hospital, agency, or school, the reporting person shall notify the person in charge of the hospital, agency, or school of his or her finding and that the report has been made, and shall make a copy of the written report available to the person in charge. One report from a hospital, agency, or school shall be considered adequate to meet the reporting requirement. A member of the staff of a hospital, agency, or school shall not be dismissed or otherwise penalized for making a report required by this act or for cooperating in an investigation.

**Content of Report:** the written report shall contain, if possible: the name of the child and a description of the abuse or neglect; the names and addresses of the child's parents, the child's guardians, the persons with whom the child resides; the child's age; and other information available to the reporting person which might establish the cause of the abuse or neglect and the manner in which the abuse or neglect occurred.

**Immunity:** M.C.L.A. 722.625

A person acting in good faith who makes a report, cooperates in an investigation, or assists in any other requirement pursuant to the reporting laws is immune from civil or criminal liability that might otherwise be incurred by that action.

**Failure to Report:** M.C.L.A. 722.633

A person who is required to report an instance of suspected child abuse or neglect, and who fails to do so is civilly liable for the damages proximately caused by the failure. A person required to report an instance of suspected child abuse or neglect, and who knowingly fails to do so is guilty of a misdemeanor punishable by imprisonment for not more than 93 days or a fine of not more than $500, or both.

**False Reporting:** M.C.L.A. 722.633

(5) A person who intentionally makes a false report of child abuse or neglect under this act knowing that the report is false is guilty of a crime as follows:

(a) If the child abuse or neglect reported would not constitute a crime or would constitute a misdemeanor if the report were true, the person is guilty of a misdemeanor punishable by imprisonment for not more than 93 days or a fine of not more than $100.00, or both.

(b) If the child abuse or neglect reported would constitute a felony if the report were true, the person is guilty of a felony punishable by the lesser of the following:

(i) The penalty for the child abuse or neglect falsely reported.

(ii) Imprisonment for not more than 4 years or a fine of not more than $2,000.00, or both.

# MINNESOTA

**Definitions:** M.S.A. § 626.556
**Neglect:** means the commission or omission of any of the acts specified under clauses (1) to (9), other than by accidental means:

(1) failure by a person responsible for a child's care to supply a child with necessary food, clothing, shelter, health, medical, or other care required for the child's physical or mental health when reasonably able to do so;

(2) failure to protect a child from conditions or actions that seriously endanger the child's physical or mental health when reasonably able to do so, including a growth delay, which may be referred to as a failure to thrive, that has been diagnosed by a physician and is due to parental neglect;

(3) failure to provide for necessary supervision or child care arrangements appropriate for a child after considering factors as the child's age, mental ability, physical condition, length of absence, or environment, when the child is unable to care for the child's own basic needs or safety, or the basic needs or safety of another child in their care;

(4) failure to ensure that the child is educated as defined in sections 120A.22 and 260C.163, subdivision 11, which does not include a parent's refusal to provide the parent's child with sympathomimetic medications, consistent with section 125A.091, subdivision 5;

(5) nothing in this section shall be construed to mean that a child is neglected solely because the child's parent, guardian, or other person responsible for the child's care in good faith selects and depends upon spiritual means or prayer for treatment or care of disease or remedial care of the child in lieu of medical care; except that a parent, guardian, or caretaker, or a person mandated to report pursuant to subdivision 3, has a duty to report if a lack of medical care may cause serious danger to the child's health. This section does not impose upon persons, not otherwise legally responsible for providing a child with necessary food, clothing, shelter, education, or medical care, a duty to provide that care;

(6) prenatal exposure to a controlled substance, as defined in section 253B.02, subdivision 2, used by the mother for a nonmedical purpose, as evidenced by withdrawal symptoms in the child at birth, results of a toxicology test performed on the mother at delivery or the child at birth, or medical effects or developmental delays during the child's first year of life that medically indicate prenatal exposure to a controlled substance;

(7) "medical neglect" as defined in section 260C.007, subdivision 6, clause (5);

(8) chronic and severe use of alcohol or a controlled substance by a parent or person responsible for the care of the child that adversely affects the child's basic needs and safety; or

(9) emotional harm from a pattern of behavior which contributes to impaired emotional functioning of the child which may be demonstrated by a substantial and observable effect in the child's behavior, emotional response, or cognition that is not within the normal range for the child's age and stage of development, with due regard to the child's culture.

**Physical Abuse:** means any physical injury, mental injury, or threatened injury, inflicted by a person responsible for the child's care on a child other than by accidental means, or any physical or mental injury that cannot reasonably be explained by the child's history of injuries, or any aversive or deprivation procedures, or regulated interventions, that have not been authorized under section 121A.67 or 245.825.

**Sexual Abuse:** means the subjection of a child by a person responsible for the child's care, by a person who has a significant relationship to the child, as defined in section 609.341, or by a person in a position of authority, as defined in section 609.341, subdivision 10, to any act which constitutes a violation of section 609.342 (criminal sexual conduct in the first degree), 609.343 (criminal sexual conduct in the second degree), 609.344 (criminal sexual conduct in the third degree), 609.345 (criminal sexual conduct in the fourth degree), or 609.3451 (criminal sexual conduct in the fifth degree). Sexual abuse also includes any act which involves a minor which constitutes a violation of prostitution offenses under sections 609.321 to 609.324 or 617.246. Sexual abuse includes threatened sexual abuse.

**Reporting:** M.S.A. § 626.556
**Who Must Report:** (1) a professional or professional's delegate who is engaged in the practice of the healing arts, social services, hospital administration, psychological or psychiatric treatment, child care, education, correctional supervision, probation and correctional services, or law enforcement; or

(2) employed as a member of the clergy and received the information while engaged in ministerial duties, provided that a member of the clergy is not required by this subdivision to report information that is otherwise privileged under section 595.02, subdivision 1, paragraph (c).

**Circumstances:** when they know or have reason to believe a child is being neglected or physically or sexually abused or has been neglected or physically or sexually abused within the preceding three years.

**Privileged Communications:** no evidence relating to the neglect or abuse of a child or to any prior incidents of neglect or abuse involving any of the same persons accused of neglect or abuse shall be excluded in any proceeding arising out of the alleged neglect or physical or sexual abuse on the grounds of privilege.

**Procedures:** MINN. STAT. ANN. § 626.556 Subd. 3, 7, 10(b) (2008)
**Individual Responsibility:** any mandated reporter who knows or has reason to believe a child is being neglected or physically or sexually abused, as defined above, or has been neglected or physically abused within the preceding three years shall immediately report to the local welfare agency, police department, or the county sheriff.

An oral report shall be made immediately by telephone or otherwise. An oral report made by a mandated reporter shall be followed within 72 hours, exclusive of weekends and holidays, by a report in writing to the appropriate police department, the county sheriff, or local welfare agency, unless the appropriate agency has informed the reporter that the oral information does not constitute a report under the law. For purposes of this subdivision, "immediately" means as soon as possible but in no event longer than 24 hours.

A person mandated to report physical or sexual child abuse or neglect occurring with a licensed facility shall report the information to the agency responsible for licensing the facility.

**Content of Report:** any report shall be of sufficient content to identify: the child; any person believed to be responsible for the abuse or neglect of the child if the person is known; the nature and extent of the abuse or neglect; and the name and address of the reporter.

**Immunity:** MINN. STAT. ANN. § 626.556 Subd. 4 (2008)
Any person making a voluntary or mandated report under the reporting laws or assisting in an investigation or assessment is immune from any civil or criminal liability that otherwise might result from this action, provided that the report is made in good faith. This law does not provide immunity to any person for failure to make a required report or for committing neglect, physical abuse, or sexual abuse of a child.

**Failure to Report:** MINN. STAT. ANN. § 626.556 Subd. 6 (2008)
A mandated reporter who knows or has reason to believe that a child is neglected or physically or sexually abused or has been neglected or physically or sexually abused within the preceding three years and fails to report is guilty of a misdemeanor.

A parent, guardian, or caretaker who knows or reasonably should know that the child's health is in serious danger and who fails to report as required by law is guilty of a gross misdemeanor if the child suffers substantial or great bodily harm because of the lack of medical care. If the child dies because of the lack of medical care, the person is guilty of a felony and may be sentenced to imprisonment for not more than two years or to payment of a fine of not more than $4,000, or both.

The law providing that a parent, guardian, or caretaker may in good faith select and depend on spiritual means or prayer for treatment or care of a child, does not exempt a parent, guardian, or caretaker for the duty to report under this provision.

**False Reporting:** MINN. STAT. ANN. § 626.556 Subd. 5 (2008)
Any person who knowingly or recklessly makes a false report under the reporting laws shall be liable in a civil suit for any actual damages suffered by the person(s) so reported and for any punitive damages set by the court or jury, plus costs and reasonable attorney fees.

# MISSISSIPPI

**Definitions:** Miss. Code Ann. § 43-21-105 (2010)
**Abused Child:** a child whose parent, guardian, custodian or responsible person, whether legally obligated or not, has caused or allowed to be caused upon said child sexual abuse or exploitation, emotional or mental injury, non-accidental physical injury, or other maltreatment.
**Child and Youth:** are synonyms, and each means a person who has not reached his 18th birthday. A child who has not reached his 18th birthday and is on active duty for the armed services or is married is not considered a "child" or "youth" for this chapter.
**Neglected Child:** a child whose parent, guardian, or custodian or any person responsible for his care or support, neglects or refuses, when able to do so, to provide proper and necessary care or support, or education as required by law, or medical, surgical, or other care necessary for his well-being; or who is otherwise without proper care, custody, supervision, or support; or who, for any reason, lacks the special care made necessary by reason of his mental condition, whether retarded or mentally ill; or lacks the care necessary for his health, morals, or well-being.
**Sexual Abuse:** obscene or pornographic photographing, filming, or depiction of children for commercial purposes or the rape, molestation, incest, prostitution or other such forms of sexual exploitation of children under circumstances which indicate that the child's health or welfare is harmed or threatened.

**Reporting:** Miss. Code Ann. § 43-21-353 (1) (2007)
**Who Must Report:** physicians, dentists, interns, residents, nurses; public or private school employees; child care givers; psychologists, social workers; attorneys, ministers; law enforcement officers; any other persons.
**Circumstances:** when they have reasonable cause to suspect that a child is an abused or neglected child.

**Procedures:** Miss. Code Ann. § 43-21-353 (1), (3), (8) (2007)
**Individual Responsibility:** any mandated reporter having reasonable cause to suspect that a child is a neglected child or an abused child shall cause an oral report to be made immediately by telephone or otherwise and followed as soon thereafter as possible by a report in writing to the Dept. of Human Services.
**Content of Report:** any report to the Dept. of Human Services shall contain the names and addresses of the child and his parents or other person responsible for his care, if known; the child's age; the nature and extent of the child injuries, including any evidence of previous injuries; and any other information that might be helpful in establishing the cause of the injury and the identity of the perpetrator.

**Immunity:** Miss. Code Ann. § 43-21-355 (2008)
Any person participating in the making of a required report pursuant to the reporting laws or participating in a judicial proceeding resulting there from shall be presumed to be acting in good faith. Any person or institution reporting in good faith shall be immune from any civil or criminal liability that might otherwise be incurred or imposed.

**Failure to Report:**
Not specifically addressed in statute.

**False Reporting:**
Not specifically addressed in statute.

# MISSOURI

**Definitions:** Mo. Ann. Stat. § 210.110 (1), (4), (12) (2005)
**Abuse:** any physical injury, sexual abuse, or emotional abuse inflicted on a child other than by accidental means by those responsible for the child's care, custody, and control, except that discipline including spanking administered in a reasonable manner, shall not be construed as abuse.
**Child:** any person, regardless of physical or mental condition, under eighteen years of age.
**Neglect:** failure to provide, by those responsible for the care, custody, and control of the child, the proper or necessary support, education as required by law, nutrition or medical, surgical, or any other care necessary for the child's well-being.

**Reporting:** Mo. Ann. Stat. §§ 210.115 (1), 568.110 (2004).
**Who Must Report:** physicians, medical examiners, coroners, dentists, chiropractors, optometrists, podiatrists, residents, interns, nurses, hospital and clinical personnel (that are engaged in the examination, care, treatment, or research of persons), other health care practitioners; day care center workers or other child care workers, teachers, principals, other school officials; psychologists, mental health practitioners, social workers, Christian Science practitioners; juvenile officers, probation officers, parole officers, peace officers, law enforcement officials; other persons with responsibility for the care of children; commercial film and photographic print processors.
**Circumstances:** when they have reasonable cause to suspect that a child has been or may be subjected to abuse or neglect; when they observe a child being subjected to conditions or circumstances that would reasonably result in abuse or neglect.

**Procedures:** Mo. Ann. Stat. § 210.115 (1), (2), (6), (7) (2004); § 210.130 (2004)
**Individual Responsibility:** when any mandated reporter has reasonable cause to suspect or observes a child being subjected to abuse or neglect, that person shall immediately report or cause a report to be made to the Division of Family Services by telephone or otherwise.
When required to report as a staff member of a medical institution, school facility, or other agency, whether public or private, the person in charge or a designated agency shall be notified immediately. The person in charge or designated agent shall then become responsible for immediately making or causing such report to be made.
If a mandated reporter has reason to believe that the victim is a resident of another state or was injured by an act that occurred in another state, the reporter may make a report to the agency of the other state. If such agency accepts the report, no reporting to the Missouri division is required.
**Content of Report:** name and address of the child and his parents or other persons responsible; child's age, sex, race; nature and extent of injuries, including any evidence of previous injury to child or siblings; name, age, and address of perpetrator, if known; family composition; source and name/address of person making the report, his occupation, and where he can be reached; actions taken, including photographs, x-rays, removal or keeping of child; and any other helpful information.

**Immunity:** Mo. Ann. Stat. § 210.135 (2005)
Any person, official, or institution complying with the provisions of the reporting laws in the making of a report, the taking of color photographs, or the making of radiologic examinations, or both, or the removal or retaining a child pursuant to statute, or in cooperating with the division, or any other law enforcement agency, juvenile office, court, or child protective service agency of this or any other state, in any of the activities pursuant to statute, or any other allegation of child abuse, neglect or assault shall have immunity from any liability, civil or criminal, that otherwise might result by reason of such actions. Provided, however, any person, official or institution intentionally filing a false report, acting in bad faith or with ill intent, shall not have immunity from any liability, civil or criminal.
Any such person, official, or institution shall have the same immunity with respect to participation in any judicial proceeding resulting from the report.

**Failure to Report:** Mo. Ann. Stat. § 210.165 (2005)
Any person violating any provision of the reporting laws is guilty of a Class A misdemeanor.

**False Reporting:** Mo. Ann. Stat. § 210.165 (2)-(4) (2004)
Any person who intentionally files a false report of child abuse or neglect shall be guilty of a Class A misdemeanor.
Every person who has been previously convicted of making a false report to the Division of Family Services and who is subsequently convicted of making a false report is guilty of a Class D felony and shall be punished as provided by law.

Appendix A

# MONTANA

**Definitions:** MONT. CODE ANN. § 41-3-102 (3), (6), (7), (9), (19), (27), (28) (2007)
**Abused or Neglected:** the state or condition of a child who has suffered child abuse or neglect.
**Child or Youth:** any person under 18 years of age.
**Child Abuse or Neglect:** harm to a child's health or welfare; or threatened harm to a child's health or welfare, including harm or threatened harm to a child's health or welfare by the acts or omissions of a person responsible for the child's welfare.
**Emotional Abuse:** injury to the emotional well-being or intellectual or psychological capacity of a child, as evidenced by an identifiable and substantial impairment of a child's physical, mental, or emotional ability to function.
**Physical Abuse:** substantial skin bruising, internal bleeding, substantial injury to skin, subdural hematoma, intentional burns, bone fractures, extreme pain, permanent or temporary disfigurement, impairment of any bodily organ or function, or death if the injury or death is not accidental.
**Sexual Abuse:** the commission of sexual assault, sexual intercourse without consent, indecent exposure, deviate sexual conduct, or incest.
**Sexual Exploitation:** allowing, permitting, or encouraging a child to engage in a prostitution offense, or allowing, permitting, or encouraging sexual abuse of children.

**Reporting:** MONT. CODE ANN. § 41-3-201 (2007)
**Who Must Report:** physicians, residents, interns, hospital staff engaged in admission/care/treatment of persons; nurses, osteopaths, chiropractors, podiatrists, medical examiners, coroners, dentists, optometrists; any other health professionals; school teachers and officials, employees who work during school hours; operators or employees of registered/licensed day-cares, substitute care facility or other child care facility; mental health professionals; social workers; Christian Science practitioners; religious healers; foster care, residential, or institutional workers; clergy; guardian ad litem, court-appointed advocates; peace officers; other law enforcement officials.
**Circumstances:** when they know or have reasonable cause to suspect, from information received in their professional or official capacity, that a child is abused or neglected.
**Privileged Communications:** A person listed as a mandated reporter may not refuse to report on grounds of a physician–patient or similar privilege. A clergy person or priest is not required if: knowledge or suspicion of abuse/neglect came from a statement/confession made to him in his official capacity; the statement was a confidential communication from a member of his church/congregation; and the confessor does not consent to disclosure. A clergy person or priest is not required to report if confidentiality is based on canon law, church doctrine, or practice.

**Procedures:** MONT. CODE ANN. § 41-3-201 (2007); § 41-3-202 (2007)
**Individual Responsibility:** when the professionals and officials listed as mandated reporters know or have reasonable cause to suspect, as a result of information they receive in their professional or official capacity, that a child is abused or neglected, they shall report the matter promptly to the Dept. of Public Health and Human Services or its local affiliate.

Any person reporting abuse or neglect that involves acts or omissions on the part of a public or private residential institution, home, facility, or agency is responsible for ensuring that the report is made to the Dept. of Public Health and Human Services through its local office.
**Content of Report:** the reports referred to under this section must contain the names and addresses of the child and the child's parents or other persons responsible for the child's care; to the extent known, the child's age and the nature and extent of the child's injuries, including any evidence of previous injuries; any other information that the maker of the report believes might be helpful in establishing the cause of the injuries or showing the willful neglect and the identity of person(s) responsible for the injury or neglect; and the facts that led the person reporting to believe that the child has suffered injury or injuries or willful neglect, within the meaning of this chapter.

**Immunity:** MONT. CODE ANN. § 41-3-203 (1) (2007)
Anyone investigating or reporting any incident of child abuse or neglect, participating in resulting judicial proceedings, or furnishing hospital or medical records pursuant to the reporting laws is immune from any civil or criminal liability that might otherwise be incurred or imposed, unless the person was grossly negligent or acted in bad faith or with malicious intent.

**Failure to Report:** MONT. CODE ANN. § 41-3-207 (2007)
Any person, official, or institution required by law to report known or suspected child abuse or neglect who fails to do so or who prevents another person from reasonably doing so is civilly liable for the damages caused by such failure or prevention.

Any person or official required by law to report known or suspected child abuse or neglect who purposely or knowingly fails to do so or purposely or knowingly prevents another person from doing so is guilty of a misdemeanor.

**False Reporting:**
Not specifically addressed in statute.

## NEBRASKA

**Definitions:** NEB. REV. STAT. ANN. § 28-710 (2008)
**Abuse or Neglect:** knowingly, intentionally, or negligently causing or permitting a minor child to be placed in a situation that endangers his or her life or physical or mental health; cruelly confined or cruelly punished; deprived of necessary food, clothing, shelter, or care; left unattended in a motor vehicle if such minor child is six years of age or younger; sexually abused; or sexually exploited by allowing, encouraging, or forcing such person to solicit for or engage in prostitution, debauchery, public indecency, or obscene or pornographic photography, films, or depictions.
**Out-of-Home Abuse or Neglect:** abuse or neglect occurring in day care homes, foster homes, day care centers, group homes, and other child care facilities or institutions.

**Reporting:** NEB. REV. STAT. ANN. § 28-711 (1) (2008); § 28-714 (2008)
**Who Must Report:** physicians, medical institutions; nurses; school employees; social workers; any other persons.
**Circumstances:** when they have reasonable cause to believe that a child has been subjected to abuse or neglect; when they observe a child being subjected to conditions or circumstances which reasonably would result in abuse or neglect.
**Privileged Communications:** the privileged communications between patient and physician, between client and professional counselor, and between husband and wife shall not be a ground for excluding evidence in any judicial proceeding resulting from a report pursuant to the reporting laws.

**Procedures:** NEB. REV. STAT. ANN. § 28-711 (2008)
**Individual Responsibility:** when any mandated reporter has reasonable cause to believe that a child has been subjected to abuse or neglect or observes such child being subject to conditions or circumstances that reasonably would result in abuse or neglect, he or she shall report such incident or cause a report to be made to the proper law enforcement agency or to the Dept. of Health and Human Services on the toll-free number established by statute.
**Content of Report:** such report may be made orally by telephone with the caller giving his or her name and address, shall be followed by a written report, and to the extent available, shall contain the address and age of the abused or neglected child; the address of the person or persons having custody of the abused or neglected child; the nature and extent of the abuse or neglect or the conditions and circumstances which would reasonably result in such abuse or neglect; any evidence of previous abuse or neglect, including the nature and extent; and any other information which in the opinion of the person reporting may be helpful in establishing the cause of such abuse or neglect and the identity of the perpetrator or perpetrators.

**Immunity:** NEB. REV. STAT. ANN. § 28-716 (2008)
Any person participating in an investigation or the making of a report pursuant to the reporting laws or participating in a judicial proceeding resulting there from shall be immune from any civil or criminal liability that might otherwise be incurred or imposed, except for maliciously false statements.

**Failure to Report:** NEB. REV. STAT. ANN. § 28-717 (2008)
Any person who willfully fails to make any report required by the reporting laws shall be guilty of a Class III misdemeanor.

**False Reporting:**
Not specifically addressed in statute.

# NEVADA

**Definitions:** Nev. Rev. Stat. Ann. § 432B.020 (1) (2003)
**Abuse or Neglect:** non-accidental physical or mental injury; sexual abuse or exploitation; negligent or maltreatment of a child caused by a person responsible for child.
**Mental Injury:** an injury to the intellectual/psychological/emotional condition of a child, evidenced by an observable impairment of his or her ability to function within his normal range.
**Negligent Treatment or Maltreatment:** when a child is abandoned, is without proper care, supervision, and lacks the subsistence, education, shelter, medical care, etc. necessary due to the faults/neglect/refusal of the person responsible.
**Physical Injury:** includes, without limitation, sprain or dislocation; damage to cartilage; fracture of a bone or skull; intracranial hemorrhage or injury to internal organ; burn or scalding; cut, laceration, puncture or bite; perm/temp disfigurement, loss or impairment of a body part/organ.
**Sexual Abuse:** includes incest; lewdness or molestation of a child; sadomasochistic abuse; sexual assault; statutory sexual seduction; genital mutilation of a female child, aiding/participating in mutilation or removing child from this state for such purpose.
**Sexual Exploitation:** forcing/allowing a child to solicit/engage in prostitution; view pornography or film; engage in filming/recording or posing in depictions or live performances exhibiting a child's genitals or sexual conduct.

**Reporting:** Nev. Rev. Stat. Ann. § 432B.220 (2008), §432B.250
**Who Must Report:** physicians, dentists/hygienists, chiropractors, optometrists, podiatrists, medical examiners, residents, interns, professional/practical nurses, assistants, advanced EMTs, persons providing medical services licensed/certified in this state; any staff of hospitals/institutions engaged in admission, care, or treatment of persons; administrators or other persons in charge of hospitals/institutions upon notification of suspected abuse by staff; coroners; school administrators/teachers/counselors, librarians; any persons employed by facilities that furnish child care; psychiatrists, psychologists, marriage/family therapists; alcohol/drug counselors; social workers; any employee/volunteer of agencies that advise persons regarding abuse and make referrals; clergymen, practitioners of Christian Science, or religious healers (unless knowledge comes from a confession); persons licensed to conduct foster homes; law enforcement officers/employees; adult/juvenile probation officers; attorneys (unless knowledge is from client who is or may be accused of it).
**Circumstances:** when they, in their professional or occupational capacities, know or have reason to believe that a child has been abused or neglected, or have reasonable cause to believe that a child has died as a result.
**Privileged Communications:** any person required to report may not invoke any privileges granted under law for failure to report.

**Procedures:** Nev. Rev. Stat. Ann. § 432B.220 (2008)
**Individual Responsibility:** report must be made to an agency that provides protective services or to a law enforcement agency immediately, but in no event later than 24 hours after there is reason to believe that a child has been abused or neglected. Any mandated reporter who has reasonable cause to believe that a child has died as a result of abuse or neglect shall report this belief to the appropriate medical examiner or coroner. The report may be made verbally, by telephone, or otherwise.
**Content of Report:** the report must contain, if obtainable: name, address, age and sex of the child; name and address of the child's parents or other person responsible; nature and extent of the abuse or neglect; any evidence of previously known or suspected abuse or neglect of the child or his siblings; name, address and relationship, if known, of the person who is alleged to have abused or neglected the child; and any other information known to the person making the report that the agency which provides protective services considers necessary.

**Immunity:** Nev. Rev. Stat. Ann. § 432B.160 (2005)
Immunity from civil or criminal liability extends to every person who in good faith makes a report pursuant to the reporting laws; conducts an interview or allows an interview to be taken; allows or takes photographs or x-rays; refers a case or recommends the filing of a petition; or participates in a judicial proceeding resulting from a referral or recommendation. There is a presumption that a person acted in good faith in any proceeding resulting from the above stated actions.

**Failure to Report:** Nev. Rev. Stat. Ann. § 432B.240 (2008)
Any person who knowingly and willfully violates the provisions of the reporting laws is guilty of a misdemeanor.

**False Reporting:**
Not specifically addressed in statute.

# NEW HAMPSHIRE

**Definitions:** N.H. Rev. Stat. Ann. § 169-C:3 (2008)
**Abandoned:** when the child has been left by his parents, guardian or custodian, w/o provision for care, supervision, or financial support although financially able.
**Abused Child:** any child who has been sexually abused or intentionally physically injured or psychologically injured so that child exhibits emotional problems generally recognized from consistent mistreatment or neglect; or physically injured by other than accidental means.
**Child:** any person who has not reached his or her 18th birthday.
**Neglected Child:** a child who has been abandoned; or who is w/o proper parental care or control, subsistence, education as required by law, or care necessary for his physical, mental, or emotional health, when established that his health has, or is likely to, suffer serious impairment; and the deprivation is not due primarily to lack of financial means, or when parents are unable to discharge responsibilities because of incarceration, hospitalization, or physical or mental incapacity.
**Sexual Abuse:** means the following activities that indicate that the child's health or welfare is harmed or threatened with harm: the employment, inducement, or coercion of any child to engage in, or assist any person to engage in, any sexually explicit conduct or simulation for the purpose of producing any visual depiction of such conduct; or the rape, molestation, incest, prostitution, or other form of sexual exploitation of children.

**Reporting:** N.H. Rev. Stat. Ann. § 169-C:29. –C:32 (2009)
**Who Must Report:** physicians, surgeons, county medical examiners, psychiatrists, residents, interns, dentists, osteopaths, optometrists, chiropractors, registered nurses, hospital personnel (engaged in admission, examination, care, and treatment of persons); teachers, school officials, school nurses, school counselors, daycare workers, any other child or foster care workers, social workers; psychologists, therapists, Christian Science practitioners, priests, ministers, rabbis; law enforcement officials; any other persons.
**Circumstances:** when they have reason to suspect that a child has been abused or neglected.
**Privileged Communications:** the privilege quality of communication between a husband and wife or any professional person and his or her patient or client, except that between attorney and client, shall not constitute grounds for failure to report.

**Procedures:** N.H. Rev. Stat. Ann. § 169-C:30 (2009)
**Individual Responsibility:** an oral report shall be made immediately by telephone or otherwise, and followed within 48 hours by a report in writing, if so requested, to the Dept. of Health and Human Services.
**Content of Report:** such report shall, if known, contain the name and address of the child suspected of being neglected or abused and the person responsible for the child's welfare, the specific information indicating neglect or the nature and extent of the child's injuries (including any evidence of previous injuries), the identity of the person or persons suspected of being responsible for such neglect or abuse, and any other information that might be helpful in establishing neglect or abuse or that may be required by the Department.

**Immunity:** N.H. Rev. Stat. Ann. § 169-C:31 (2009)
Anyone participating in good faith in the making of a report pursuant to the reporting laws is immune from any civil or criminal liability that might otherwise be incurred or imposed. Any such participant has the same immunity with respect to participation in any investigation by the Division for Children, Youth, and Families, or judicial proceeding resulting from such report.

**Failure to Report:** N.H. Rev. Stat. Ann. § 169-C:39 (2009)
Anyone who knowingly violates any provision of the reporting laws shall be guilty of a misdemeanor.

**False Reporting:**
Not specifically addressed in statute.

# NEW JERSEY

**Definitions:** N.J. Stat. Ann. § 9:6–8.9 (a)-(c) (2009)
**Abused Child:** a child under 18 years whose parent, guardian, or other person having his custody and control inflicts or allows to be inflicted upon such child physical injury by other than accidental means which causes or creates a substantial risk of death, or serious disfigurement or impairment of physical or emotional health or loss or impairment of any bodily organ; creates or allows to be created a substantial or ongoing risk of physical injury to such child by other than accidental means which would be likely to cause death or serious disfigurement, loss or impairment of the function of any bodily organ; or commits or allows to be committed an act of sexual abuse against the child; or a child whose physical, mental, or emotional condition has been impaired or is in imminent danger of becoming impaired as the result of a failure to exercise a minimum degree of care in supplying adequate food, clothing, shelter, medical or surgical care, although financially or by other means, able to do so, or in providing proper supervision, by inflicting or allowing to be inflicted harm, or substantial risk thereof, including excessive corporal punishment or physical restraint, or any other act of a serious nature requiring the aid of the court; or a child who has been willfully abandoned; or who is in an institution, except day schools, and has been placed inappropriately with knowledge that the placement has resulted in harm to the child's mental or physical well-being, or has been willfully isolated from ordinary social contact.

**Reporting:** N.J. Stat. Ann. § 9:6–8.10 (2009)
**Who Must Report:** any person.
**Circumstances:** any person having reasonable cause to believe that a child has been subjected to child abuse or acts of child abuse shall report the same immediately to the Division of Youth and Family Services by telephone or otherwise.

**Procedures:** N.J. Stat. Ann. § 9:6–8.10 (2009)
**Individual Responsibility:** any person having reasonable cause to believe that a child has been subjected to child abuse or acts of child abuse shall report the same immediately to the Division of Youth and Family Services by telephone or otherwise.
**Content of Report:** such reports, where possible, shall contain the names and addresses of the child and his parent, guardian, or other person having custody and control of the child; if known, the child's age; the nature and possible extent of the child's injuries, abuse, or maltreatment, including any evidence of previous injuries, abuse, or maltreatment; and any other information that the person believes may be helpful with respect to the child abuse and the identity of the perpetrator.

**Immunity:** N.J. Stat. Ann. § 9:6–8.13 (2009)
Anyone acting pursuant to the reporting laws in the making of a report under the reporting laws shall have immunity from any civil or criminal liability that might otherwise be incurred or imposed. Any such person shall have the same immunity with respect to testimony given in any judicial proceeding resulting from such report.

**Failure to Report:** N.J. Stat. Ann. § 9:6–8.14 (2009)
Any person knowingly violating the reporting laws, including the failure to report an act of child abuse having reasonable cause to believe that an act of child abuse has been committed, is a disorderly person and may be sentenced to imprisonment for a definite term which shall not exceed six months.

**False Reporting:**
Not specifically addressed in statute.

# NEW MEXICO

**Definitions:** N.M. STAT. ANN. § 32A-4-2 (2009)
**Abused Child:** a child who is at risk of serious harm; has suffered physical/emotional/psychological/sexual abuse or exploitation by the parent/guardian; or whose parent/guardian has knowingly or negligently endangered, tortured, or cruelly confined/punished the child.
**Neglected Child:** a child who has been abandoned or w/o proper care, subsistence, education, medical or other care due to faults or habits of the parent/guardian or by neglect or refusal, when able to provide; who has been physically/sexually abused when parent/guardian knew or should have known and failed to take reasonable protective steps, or is not responsible due to incarceration, hospitalization, or physical/mental disorder; or a child placed for care or adoption illegally.
**Physical Abuse:** includes, but not limited to, skin bruising/bleeding, malnutrition, failure to thrive, burns, any bone fracture, subdural hematoma, soft tissue swelling or death and there is no justifiable explanation for the condition, or it is at variance with the degree or nature of the condition, or it does not appear accidental.
**Sexual Abuse:** includes, but is not limited to, criminal sexual contact, incest, or penetration.
**Sexual Exploitation:** includes, but not limited to, allowing or encouraging a child to engage in prostitution, obscene or pornographic photographing, or filming for commercial purposes.

**Reporting:** N.M. STAT. ANN. § 32A-4-3 (A) (2005); § 32A-4-5 (A) (2005)
**Who Must Report:** every person; licensed physicians, residents or interns examining, attending or treating a child; law enforcement officers; judges presiding during any proceeding; registered nurses; visiting nurses; schoolteachers or school officials; or social workers.
**Circumstances:** any mandated reporter, acting in an official capacity, who knows or has a reasonable suspicion that a child is an abused or neglected child.
**Privileged Communications:** in any proceeding alleging neglect or abuse under law resulting from a report required, or in any proceeding in which that report or any of its contents are sought to be introduced in evidence, the report or its contents or any other facts related thereto or to the condition of the child who is the subject of the report shall not be excluded on the ground that the matter is or may be the subject of a physician–patient privilege or similar privilege or rule against disclosure.

**Procedures:** N.M. STAT. ANN. § 32A-4-3 (A)-(D) (2005)
**Individual Responsibility:** any mandated reporter shall report a matter of child abuse or neglect immediately to a local law enforcement agency, the Child, Youth and Families Department's office in the county agency where the child resides, or tribal law enforcement or social services for any Indian residing in Indian country.
 The written report shall be submitted upon a standardized form agreed to by the law enforcement agency and the Children, Youth and Families Dept.
**Content of Report:** the written report shall contain the names and addresses of the child and the child's parents, guardian, or custodian; the child's age, the nature and extent of the child's injuries, including any evidence of previous injuries, other information that the maker of the report believes might be helpful in establishing the cause of the injuries and the identity of the person responsible for the injuries.

**Immunity:** N.M. STAT. ANN. § 32A-4-5 (B) (2005)
 Anyone reporting an instance of alleged child neglect or abuse or participating in a judicial proceeding brought as a result of a report required by the reporting laws is presumed to be acting in good faith and shall be immune from civil or criminal liability that might otherwise be incurred or imposed by the law unless the person acted in bad faith or with malicious purpose.

**Failure to Report:** N.M. STAT. ANN. § 32A-4-3 (F) (2005)
 Any person who violates a provision of the reporting laws is guilty of a misdemeanor and shall be sentenced pursuant to law.

**False Reporting:**
 Not specifically addressed in statute.

Appendix A

# NEW YORK

**Definitions:** McKinney's Family Court Act § 1012 (2009)
   Abused child means a child less than eighteen years of age whose parent or other person legally responsible for his care
   (i) inflicts or allows to be inflicted upon such child physical injury by other than accidental means which causes or creates a substantial risk of death, or serious or protracted disfigurement, or protracted impairment of physical or emotional health or protracted loss or impairment of the function of any bodily organ, or
   (ii) creates or allows to be created a substantial risk of physical injury to such child by other than accidental means which would be likely to cause death or serious or protracted disfigurement, or protracted impairment of physical or emotional health or protracted loss or impairment of the function of any bodily organ, or
   (iii) commits, or allows to be committed an offense against such child defined in article one hundred thirty of the penal law (referring to sex offenses including sexual intercourse and sexual contact); allows, permits or encourages such child to engage in any act described in sections 230.25 (promoting prostitution in the third degree), 230.30 (promoting prostitution in the second degree) and 230.32 of the penal law (promoting prostitution in the second degree); commits any of the acts described in sections 255.25 (incest in the third degree), 255.26 (incest in the second degree) and 255.27 of the penal law (incest in the first degree); or allows such child to engage in acts or conduct described in article two hundred sixty-three of the penal law provided, however, that (a) the corroboration requirements contained in the penal law and (b) the age requirement for the application of article two hundred sixty-three of such law shall not apply to proceedings under this article.

**Reporting:** N.Y. Soc. Serv. Law § 413 (1) (2009)
**Who Must Report:** physicians; registered physician assistants; surgeons; medical examiners; coroners; dentists; dental hygienists; osteopaths; optometrists; chiropractors; podiatrists; residents; interns; registered nurses; hospital personnel engaged in the admission, examination, care or treatment of persons; or a Christian Science practitioner; school officials; social services workers; day care center workers; providers of family or group family day care; employees or volunteers in a residential care facility; or any other child care or foster care worker; psychologists; mental health professionals; substance abuse counselors; or alcoholism counselors; peace officers; police officers; district attorneys; investigators employed in the office of a district attorney; or other law enforcement officials.
**Circumstances:** when they have reasonable cause to suspect that a child coming before them in their professional or official capacities is an abused or maltreated child; or when they have reasonable cause to suspect that a child is an abused or maltreated child where the parent, guardian, custodian, or other person legally responsible for such child comes before them in their professional or official capacities and states from personal knowledge facts, conditions or circumstances which, if correct, would render the child an abused or maltreated child.

**Procedures:** N.Y. Soc. Serv. Law § 415 (2008); § 413 (1) (2009)
**Individual Responsibility:** reports shall be made immediately by telephone or by telephone facsimile on a form supplied by the commissioner. Oral reports shall be followed by a report in writing within 48 hours of the oral report. When required to report as a member of the staff of a medical or other public or private institution, school, facility, or agency, he or she shall immediately notify the person in charge of such establishment, who then also shall become responsible to report or cause reports to be made.
**Content of Report:** the written reports on forms supplied by the commissioner shall include the names and addresses of the child and his/her parents or other persons responsible for his/her care, if known, and, as the case may be, the name and address of the residential care facility or program in which the child resides or is receiving care; the child's age, sex and race; the nature and extent of the injuries, abuse or maltreatment, including any prior injury to the child, or his/her siblings; the name of the person(s) alleged to be responsible for the injury, abuse or maltreatment, if known; family composition, where appropriate; the source and the person making the report and where he or she can be reached; the actions taken by the reporter, including taking pictures and x-rays, removing or keeping of the child or notifying the medical examiner or coroner; and any other information the commissioner requires or the reporter believes may be helpful.

**Immunity:** N.Y. Soc. Serv. Law § 419 (2009)
   Any person, official, or institution participating in good faith in the making of a report or the taking of photographs, the removal or keeping of a child pursuant to this title or the disclosure of child protective services information in compliance with child reporting laws shall have immunity from any civil or criminal liability that might otherwise result by reason of such actions.
   For the purpose of any civil or criminal proceeding, the good faith of any such person, official, or institution required to report cases of child abuse or maltreatment or providing a reporting procedure service shall be presumed, provided such person, official, or institution was acting in the discharge of their duties and within the scope of their employment and that such liability did not result from the willful misconduct or gross negligence of such person, official, or institution.

**Failure to Report:** N.Y. Soc. Serv. Law § 420 (1)-(2) (2009)
   Any person, official, or institution required by the reporting laws to report a case of suspected child abuse or maltreatment who willfully fails to do so shall be guilty of a Class A misdemeanor.
   Any person, official, or institution required by the reporting laws to report a case of suspected child abuse or maltreatment who knowingly and willfully fails to do so shall be civilly liable for the damages proximately caused by such failure.

**False Reporting:** N.Y. Penal Law § 240.55 (2008)
   A person is guilty of falsely reporting an incident in the second degree when knowing the information reported conveyed or circulated to be false or baseless, he or she reports, by word or action, to the statewide central register of child abuse and maltreatment, an alleged occurrence or condition of child abuse or maltreatment which did not if fact occur or exist.
   Falsely reporting an incident in the second degree is a Class A misdemeanor.

## NORTH CAROLINA

**Definitions:** N.C. Gen. Stat. § 7B-101 (2009)
**Abused Juveniles:** any juvenile less than 18 whose parent, guardian, or caretaker inflicts, allows to be inflicted, creates or allows to be created a serious physical injury or risk of physical injury by other than accidental means; uses or allows cruel or grossly inappropriate procedures or devices to modify behavior; commits, permits, or encourages the commission of a violation upon a juvenile- 1st/2nd degree rape; 1st/2nd degree sexual offense; sexual act by a custodian; crime against nature; incest; preparation of obscene photographs, slides, or motion pictures of juveniles; employing or permitting the juvenile to violate obscenity laws; providing obscene material to the juvenile; 1st/2nd degree sexual exploitation; promoting the prostitution of or taking indecent liberties with the juvenile; creates or allows to be created serious emotional damage evidenced by severe anxiety, depression, withdrawal, or aggressive behavior toward self or others; encourages or approves of acts involving moral turpitude.
**Juvenile:** a person who has not reached his 18th birthday, and is not married, emancipated, or a member of the U.S. armed forces.
**Neglected Juvenile:** a juvenile who does not receive proper care, supervision, or discipline from parent/guardian; who has been abandoned; who is not provided necessary medical and remedial care; who lives in an environment injurious to the juvenile's welfare; or who has been place for care or adoption illegally.

**Reporting:** N.C. Gen. Stat. § 7B-301 (2005); § 7B-310 (2005)
**Who Must Report:** any persons or institutions.
**Circumstances:** when they have cause to suspect that any juvenile is abused, neglected, dependent, or has died as a result of maltreatment.
**Privileged Communications:** no privilege shall be grounds for any person or institution failing to report that a juvenile may have been abused, neglected, or dependent, even if the knowledge or suspicion is acquired in an official professional capacity, except when the knowledge is gained by an attorney from that attorney's client during representation only in the abuse, neglect, or dependency case.

**Procedures:** N.C. Gen. Stat. § 7B-301 (2005)
**Individual Responsibility:** any person or institution who has cause to believe that any juvenile is abused, neglected, or dependent, or has died as the result of maltreatment, shall report the case of that juvenile to the director of the Dept. of Social Services in the county where the juvenile resides or is found. The report may be made orally, by telephone, or in writing.
**Content of Report:** the report shall include information as is known to the person making it, including: the name and address of the juvenile; the name and address of the juvenile's parent, guardian, or caretaker; the age of the juvenile; the names and ages of other juveniles in the home; the present whereabouts of the juvenile if not at the home address; the nature and extent of any injury or condition resulting from abuse, neglect, or dependency; and any other information that the person making the report believes might be helpful in establishing the need for protective services or court intervention.
If the report is made orally or by telephone, the person making the report shall give his or her name, address, and telephone number. Refusal of the person making the report to give a name shall not preclude the Dept.'s investigation or the alleged abuse, neglect, dependency, or death as a result of maltreatment.

**Immunity:** N.C. Gen. Stat. § 7B-309 (2005)
Anyone who makes a report pursuant to the reporting laws, cooperates with the County Dept. of Social Services in a protective services inquiry or investigation, testifies in any judicial proceeding resulting from a protective services report or investigation, or otherwise participates in the program authorized by law is immune from any civil or criminal liability that might otherwise be incurred or imposed for such action, provided that the person was acting in good faith.
In any proceeding involving liability, good faith is presumed.

**Failure to Report:**
Not specifically addressed in statute.

**False Reporting:**
Not specifically addressed in statute.

# NORTH DAKOTA

**Definitions:** N.D. Cent. Code § 50-25.1-02 (2007)
**Abused Child:** an individual under the age of 18 years who is suffering from serious physical harm or traumatic abuse caused by other than accidental means by a person responsible for the child's welfare, or who is suffering from or was subjected to any act involving that individual in violation of section 12.1-20-01 through 12.1-20-08 concerning sex offenses against children.
**Institutional Child Abuse and Neglect:** situations of known or suspected child abuse or neglect where the person responsible for the child's welfare is an employee of a residential child care facility, a treatment or care center for mentally retarded, a public or private residential educational facility, a maternity home, or any residential facility owned or managed by the state or a political subdivision of the state.
**Neglected Child:** a deprived child as defined in chapter 27-20.

**Reporting:** N.D. Cent. Code § 50-25.1-03, -10 (2007)
**Who Must Report:** physicians; nurses; dentists; optometrists; medical examiners or coroners; or any other medical or mental health professional or religious practitioner of the healing arts; schoolteacher or administrator; school counselor; addiction counselor; social worker; day care center or any other child care worker; police or law enforcement officer, or member of the clergy.
**Circumstances:** when they have knowledge of or reasonable cause to suspect that a child is abused or neglected or has died as a result of abuse or neglect. They shall report the circumstances to the department if the knowledge or suspicion is derived from information received by that person in that person's official or professional capacity.
**Privileged Communications:** A member of the clergy, however, is not required to report such circumstance if the knowledge or suspicion is derived from information received in the capacity of a spiritual adviser.
Any privilege of communication between husband and wife or between any professional person and the person's patient or client, except between attorney and client, is abrogated and does not constitute grounds for preventing a report to be made or for excluding evidence in any proceeding regarding child abuse, neglect, or death resulting from abuse or neglect resulting from a report made under this chapter.

**Procedures:** N.D. Cent. Code § 50-25.1-04 (2008)
**Individual Responsibility:** all persons mandated or permitted to report cases of known or suspected child abuse or neglect shall immediately cause oral or written reports to be made to the Department or the Department's designee. Oral reports must be followed by written reports within 48 hours if so requested by the Department.

Reports involving known or suspected institutional child abuse or neglect must be made and received in the same manner as all other reports made under this chapter.
**Content of Report:** a requested written report must include information specifically sought by the Department if the reporter possesses or has reasonable access to that information.

**Immunity:** N.D. Cent. Code § 50-25.1-09 (2008)
Any person, other than the alleged violator, participating in good faith in the making of a report, assisting in an investigation or assessment, furnishing information, providing protective services or who is a member of the child fatality review panel is immune from any civil or criminal liability, except for criminal liability as provided for under penalties for failure to report and false reporting, that otherwise might result from reporting the alleged case of abuse, neglect, or death resulting from child abuse or neglect.

A person would not be immune from criminal liability for failure to report or for false reporting.

For the purpose of any civil or criminal proceeding, the good faith of any person required to report cases of child abuse, neglect or death is presumed.

**Failure to Report:** N.D. Cent. Code § 50-25.1-13 (2009)
Any person required by this chapter to report or to supply information concerning a case of known or suspected child abuse, neglect, or death resulting from abuse or neglect who willfully, as defined in section 12.1-02-02, fails to do so is guilty of a Class B misdemeanor.

**False Reporting:** N.D. Cent. Code § 50-25.1-13 (2009)
Any person who willfully makes a false report or provides false information which causes a report to be made, under this chapter is guilty of a Class B misdemeanor unless the false report is made to a law enforcement official, in which case the person who causes the report to be made is guilty of a Class A misdemeanor.

A person who willfully makes a false report, or willfully provides false information that causes a report to be made, under this chapter is also liable in a civil action for all damages suffered by the person reported, including exemplary damages.

# OHIO

**Definitions:** Ohio Rev. Code Ann. §§ 2151.030- 031, (2006)
**Abused Child:** any child who is a victim of sexual activity, as defined in 2907.01, where such activity would constitute an offense, except that the court need not find that any person has been convicted of the offense; is endangered, except that the court need not find that any person has been convicted of the offense; exhibits evidence of any physical or mental injury or death, inflicted by other than accidental means, or an injury or death which is at variance with the history given it; because of the acts of his parents/guardian the child suffers physical or mental injury that harms or threatens to harm the child's health or welfare; is subjected to out-of-home-care child abuse.
**Neglected Child:** any child who is abandoned by his parents/guardian; who lacks proper parental care because of the faults or habits of his parents/guardian; whose parents/guardian neglects or refuses to provide him with proper or necessary subsistence, education, or medical or surgical care or treatment, or other care necessary for his health, morals, or well-being; whose parents/guardian have placed or attempted to place him in violation of statutes regarding the placement and adoption of children; who, because of the omission of his parents/guardian, suffers physical or mental injury that harms or threatens to harm the child's health or welfare; who is subjected to out-of-home-care child neglect.

**Reporting:** OHIO REV. CODE ANN. § 2151.421 (2008)
**Who Must Report:** physicians, hospital intern/resident; dentists; podiatrists; practitioners of medicine/surgery; registered/licensed practical/visiting nurses; other health care professionals; speech pathologists; audiologists; coroners; licensed/school psychologists; administrators or employees of daycare centers, certified agencies, other children services; day/residential camps; school teachers/employees/authorities; social workers; licensed professional counselors; spiritual healers by prayer of a recognized religion; attorneys.
**Circumstances:** when acting in an official or professional capacity, one knows or suspects that a child under 18 or a physically/mentally handicapped child under 21 has suffered or faces a threat of suffering physical/mental injury or condition that reasonably indicates abuse or neglect.
**Privileged Communications:** an attorney/physician is not required to report attorney–client/physician–patient communications if they could not testify about them in a civil or criminal proceeding, except client waives privilege (and attorney/physician shall make a report) if client is under 18 or 21, if physically/mentally handicapped; if the attorney/physician knows or suspects that client has suffered or faces a threat of suffering injury; and relationship does not arise out of client attempting to have an abortion w/o parental notification. The physician–patient privilege shall not exclude evidence on injuries in a judicial proceeding.

**Procedures:** OHIO REV. CODE ANN. § 2151.421 (2008)
**Individual Responsibility:** no person designated as a mandatory reporter who is acting in an official or professional capacity and knows or suspects that a child under 18, or a mentally retarded, developmentally disabled or physically impaired child under 21 has suffered or faces threat of suffering any physical or mental wound, injury, disability, or condition of a nature that reasonably indicates abuse or neglect of the child shall fail to immediately report that knowledge or suspicion to the public children services agency or municipal or county police officer in the county in which the child resides or in which the abuse or neglect is occurring or has occurred. Any report shall be made forthwith either by telephone or in person and shall be followed by a written report if requested by the receiving agency or officer.
**Content of Report:** the written report shall contain the names and addresses of the child and the child's parents or the person(s) having custody of the child, if known; the child's age and the nature and extent of the child's known or suspected injuries, abuse or neglect or of the known or suspected threat of injury, abuse, or neglect, including any evidence of previous injuries, abuse, or neglect; and any other information that might be helpful in establishing the cause of the known or suspected injury, abuse, or neglect or threat thereof.

**Immunity:** OHIO REV. CODE ANN. § 2151.421 (G)(1) (2008)
Except as provided in the law regarding false reports, anyone or any hospital, institution, school, health department, or agency participating in the making of reports under the reporting laws and anyone participating in good faith in a judicial proceeding resulting from the reports shall be immune from any civil or criminal liability for injury, death, or loss to person or property that otherwise might be incurred or imposed as a result of the making of the reports or the participation in the judicial proceeding.

**Failure to Report:**
Not specifically addressed in statute.

**False Reporting:** OHIO REV. CODE ANN. § 2921.14 (2008)
A person who knowingly makes or causes another to make a false report that alleges that any person has committed an act or omission that resulted in a child being an abused child or neglected child is guilty of a violation of § 2921.14 below.
No person shall knowingly make or cause another person to make a false report alleging that any person has committed an act or omission that resulted in a child being an abused child or a neglected child.
Whoever violates this section is guilty of making or causing a false report of child abuse or child neglect, a misdemeanor of the first degree.

# OKLAHOMA

**Definitions:** 10A Okl. Stat. Ann. §1–1–105 (2009)
**Abuse:** harm or threatened harm to a child's health or safety by a person responsible for the child's health or safety, including sexual abuse and sexual exploitation.
**Child:** any person under the age of 18.
**Harm or Threatened Harm:** includes, but is not limited to non-accidental physical or mental injury, sexual abuse, sexual exploitation, neglect, or dependency.
**Neglect:** failure or omission to provide adequate food, clothing, shelter, medical care, and supervision, or special care made necessary by the physical or mental condition of the child.

**Reporting:** Okl. Stat. Ann. §1–2–101 (2009)
**Who Must Report:** Every person having reason to believe that a child under the age of eighteen (18) years is a victim of abuse or neglect shall report the matter promptly to the Department of Human Services. Reports shall be made to the hotline provided for in subsection A of this section. Any allegation of abuse or neglect reported in any manner to a county office shall immediately be referred to the hotline by the Department.
**Circumstances:** when they have reason to believe that a child is a victim of abuse or neglect; when a health care professional examines, attends, or treats the victim of what appears to be criminally injurious conduct, including, but not limited to, child physical or sexual abuse.
**Privileged Communications:** No privilege or contract shall relieve any person from the requirement of reporting pursuant to this section.

**Procedures:** Okl. Stat. Ann. §1–2–101 (2009)
**Individual Responsibility:** The reporting obligations are individual, and no employer or administrator shall impede or inhibit the reporting obligations of any employee or other person. Internal procedures of reporting child abuse may be established but shall not relieve the employee or other such person from the individual reporting obligations.
**Content of Report:** if the report is not written, it shall be reduced to writing by the Dept. of Human Services, as soon as may be after made by phone or otherwise. The report shall contain names and addresses of the child and the child's parents or other persons responsible for the child; child's age; nature and extent of the abuse or neglect, including any evidence of any previous injuries; nature and extent of the child's dependence on a controlled or dangerous substance; and any information that the reporter believes might be helpful in establishing the cause of the injuries and the identity of the person(s) responsible, if known.

**Immunity:** 10A Okl. Stat. Ann. §1–2–104 (2009)
Any person, in good faith and exercising due care, participating in the making of a report pursuant to reporting laws or allowing access to a child by persons authorized to investigate a report concerning the child shall have immunity from any civil or criminal liability that might otherwise be incurred or imposed. Any such participant shall have immunity with respect to participation in any judicial proceeding resulting from such report.

**Failure to Report:** Okl. Stat. Ann. §1–2–101 (2009)
Any person who knowingly and willfully fails to promptly report any incident of child abuse or neglect may be reported by the Dept. of Human Services to local law enforcement for criminal investigation and, upon conviction thereof, shall be guilty of a misdemeanor.

**False Reporting:** Okl. Stat. Ann. §1–2–101 (2009)
Any person who knowingly and willfully makes a false report under the reporting laws or a report that the person knows lacks factual foundation may be reported to local law enforcement for a criminal investigation and, upon conviction thereof, shall be guilty of a misdemeanor.

If a court determines that an accusation of child abuse or neglect made during custody proceedings is false and the person making the accusation knew it to be false at the time the accusation was made, the court may impose a fine, not to exceed $5,000 and reasonable attorney fees incurred, against the person making the accusation. This remedy is in addition to the paragraph above or to any other remedy provided by law.

# OREGON

**Definitions:** Or. Rev. Stat. § 419B.005 (1), (2) (2005)
**Abuse:** any assault and any physical injury to a child that has been caused by other than accidental means, including injury which appears to be at variance with the explanation given; any mental injury to a child, which shall include only observable and substantial impairment of the child's mental or psychological ability to function caused by cruelty, with due regard to the child's culture; rape of a child, which includes, but is not limited to, rape, sodomy, unlawful sexual penetration and incest; sexual abuse; sexual exploitation, including, but not limited to, contributing to the sexual delinquency of a minor, any other conduct which allows, authorizes, permits or encourages a child to engage in the performing for people to observe or the photographing, filming, tape recording, or other exhibition which, in whole or in part, depicts sexual conduct or contact, child sexual abuse or child rape, but not including any conduct that is part of any child abuse investigation or which is designed to serve education or legitimate purposes; encouraging or hiring a child into prostitution; negligent or maltreatment of a child, including, but not limited to, the failure to provide adequate food, clothing, shelter, or medical care; threatened harm to a child, subjecting substantial risk of harm to the child's health or welfare; or buying or selling a person under 18.
**Child:** an unmarried person who is under 18 years of age.

**Reporting:** Or. Rev. Stat. § 419B.005 (3) (2005); § 419B.010 (1) (2005)
**Who Must Report:** any public or private official; physicians, including interns or residents; dentists; licensed practical nurses or registered nurses; optometrists; chiropractors; or naturopathic physicians; school employees; employees of the Dept. of Human Resources, county health departments, community mental health programs and developmental disabilities programs, county juvenile departments, licensed child-caring agencies, or alcohol and drug treatment programs; psychologists; clergymen; licensed clinical social workers; child care or foster care providers; licensed professional counselors; or licensed marriage and family therapists; peace officers; attorneys; firefighters or emergency medical technicians; or court-appointed special advocates.
**Circumstances:** when they have reasonable cause to believe that any child with whom they come in contact has suffered abuse or that any person with whom they come in contact has abused a child.
**Privileged Communications:** nothing shall affect the duty to report imposed by this section, except that a psychiatrist, psychologist, clergyman, or attorney shall not be required to report such information communicated by a person if the communication is privileged under law.

**Procedures:** Or. Rev. Stat. § 419B.015 (2008)
**Individual Responsibility:** a person making a report of child abuse, whether voluntarily or pursuant to mandatory reporter law, shall make an oral report by telephone or otherwise to the local office of the State Office for Services to Children and Families, the designee of the State Office for Services to Children and Families, or a law enforcement agency within the county where the person making the report is located at the time of the contact.
**Content of Report:** such report shall contain, if known: names and addresses of the child and the parents of the child or other persons responsible for the care of the child; child's age; nature and extent of abuse, including any evidence of previous abuse; explanation given for abuse; and any other information that the person making the report believes might be helpful in establishing the cause of the abuse and the identity of the perpetrator.

**Immunity:** Or. Rev. Stat. § 419B.025 (2008)
Anyone participating in good faith in the making of a report of child abuse and who has reasonable grounds for the making thereof shall have immunity from any civil or criminal liability that might otherwise be incurred or imposed with respect to the making or content of such report. Any such participant shall have the same immunity with respect to participating in any judicial proceeding resulting from such report.

**Failure to Report:** Or. Rev. Stat. § 419B.010 (2) (2005)
Prosecution for failing to report when required to report by law is a class A violation and shall be commenced at anytime within 18 months after the commission of the offense.

**False Reporting:**
Not specifically addressed in statute.

# PENNSYLVANIA

**Definitions:** 23 Pa. Cons. Stat. Ann. § 6303 (a)-(b) (2008)
Child Abuse: any recent act or failure to act by a perpetrator which causes non-accidental serious physical injury, serious mental injury, sexual abuse or sexual exploitation to a child under 18. Any recent act, failure to act, or series of acts or failures which creates an imminent risk of serious physical injury, sexual abuse, or sexual exploitation of a child under 18. Serious physical neglect constituting prolonged/repeated lack of supervision or the failure to provide essentials of life, including medical care, which endangers a child's life, development, or functioning.
Serious Bodily Injury: injury that creates a substantial risk of death or causes serious permanent disfigurement or loss/impairment of function of any bodily organ.
Serious Mental Injury: a psychological condition, diagnosed by a physician or licensed psychologist that renders a child chronically and severely anxious, agitated, depressed, socially withdrawn, psychotic or in reasonable fear that life is threatened; or seriously interferes with a child's ability to have age-appropriate development/tasks.
Serious Physical Injury: injury causing severe pain or impairing significant physical functioning.
Sexual Abuse or Exploitation: the employment, persuasion, or coercion of a child to engage or assist in any sexually explicit conduct or any simulation of any sexually explicit conduct for any visual depiction.

**Reporting:** 23 Pa. Cons. Stat. Ann. § 6311 (a)-(b) (2007)
Who Must Report: licensed physicians, osteopaths, medical examiners, coroners, funeral directors, dentists, optometrists, chiropractors, podiatrists, interns, registered nurses, licensed practical nurses, hospital personnel engaged in the admission, examination, care or treatment of persons, Christian Science practitioners; members of the clergy, school administrators, school teachers, school nurses, social services workers, daycare center workers or any other child-care or foster care workers, mental health professionals, peace officers, or law enforcement officials.
Circumstances: when, in the course of their employment, occupation, or practice of their profession, they come into contact with children who they have reasonable cause to suspect, on the basis of their professional experience, that a child coming before them is an abused child.
Privileged Communications: except with respect to confidential communications made to an ordained member of the clergy, which are protected under law, the privileged communication between any professional person required to report and the patient or client of that person shall not apply to situations involving child abuse and shall not constitute grounds for failure to report as required by this chapter.

**Procedures:** 23 Pa. Cons. Stat. Ann. § 6311 (2007); § 6313 (a)-(d) (2007)
Individual Responsibility: reports from persons required to report shall be made immediately by telephone to the Department, and may be made to the appropriate county agency; and in writing within 48 hours after the oral report. Whenever required to report as a member of the staff of a medical or other public or private institution, school, facility or agency, that person shall immediately notify the person in charge or the designated agent of the person in charge. Upon notification, the person in charge or designated agent, shall assume responsibility and legal obligation to report or cause a report to be made in accordance with law.
Content of Report: written reports shall be made on department forms, and include the following, if available: names and addresses of child and parent or other person responsible for the care of the child, if known; where the suspected abuse occurred; age and sex of the subjects of the report; nature and extent of the suspected child abuse, including any evidence of prior abuse to the child or siblings of the child; name and relationship of the person(s) responsible for the suspected abuse, if known, and any evidence of prior abuse by that person; family composition; sources of the report; person making the report and when/where that person can be reached; actions taken by the reporter, including taking pictures/x-rays, removing or keeping the child or notifying a medical examiner/coroner; and any information the department requires.

**Immunity:** 23 Pa. Cons. Stat. Ann. § 6318 (a)-(b) (2008)

A person, hospital, institution, school, facility, agency, or agency employee that participates in good faith in the making of a report, cooperating with an investigation, testifying in a proceeding arising out of an instance of suspected child abuse, or the taking of photographs, or the removal or keeping of a child pursuant to child custody law, and any official or employee of a county agency who refers a report of suspected abuse to law enforcement authorities or provides services under this law shall have immunity from civil and criminal liability that might otherwise result by reason of those actions.

For the purpose of any civil or criminal proceeding, the good faith of a person required to report pursuant to child abuse reporting laws and of any person required to make a referral to law enforcement officers under this law shall be presumed.

**Failure to Report:** 23 Pa. Cons. Stat. Ann. § 6319 (2007)

A person or official required by the reporting laws to report a case of suspected child abuse who willfully fails to do so commits a summary offense for the first violation and a misdemeanor of the third degree for a second or subsequent violation.

**False Reporting:**
Not specifically addressed in statute.

# RHODE ISLAND

**Definitions:** R.I. Gen. Laws § 40-11-2 (2006)
**Abused and Neglected Child:** a child whose physical or mental health or welfare is harmed or threatened when his parent or other person responsible for his welfare inflicts, or allows to be inflicted, physical/mental injury, including excessive corporal punishment; or creates, or allows to be created, a substantial risk thereof; or commits or allows an act of sexual abuse; or fails to supply the child with adequate food, clothing, shelter, or medical care, though financially able or offered reasonable means; or fails to provide a minimum degree of care or supervision because of unwillingness or inability caused by, social/psychiatric problems, mental incompetence, or drug/alcohol use to the extent that one loses ability; or abandons/deserts the child; or sexually exploits the child by permitting/encouraging prostitution or pornographic photographing, filming, or depiction of the child in any sexual act; or commits a sexual offense or sexual penetration against child.
**Child:** a person under 18 years.
**Mental Injury:** a substantially diminished psychological or intellectual functioning in relation to, but not limited to, such factors as failure to thrive, ability to think, control of aggressive or self-destructive impulses, acting-out (including incorrigibility, un-governability or habitual truancy), provided that the injury is attributable to an unwillingness or inability of a parent or person responsible to exercise a minimum degree of care.

**Reporting:** R.I. Gen. Laws § 40-11-3 (a)-(c) (2008); § 40-11-6 (a) (2008); § 40-11-11 (2008)
**Who Must Report:** any persons; any physician or duly certified registered nurse practitioner.
**Circumstances:** when they have reasonable cause to know or suspect that any child has been abused or neglected, has been a victim of sexual abuse by another child, or is suffering from a sexually transmitted disease. When parents of an infant have requested deprivation of nutritional, medical, or surgical intervention that is necessary to sustain life or ameliorate a life-threatening medical condition, if intervention is generally provided to similarly conditioned infants, whether or not handicapped. This does not, however, prevent a child's parents and physician from discontinuing life-support systems or nonpalliative treatments when, in the opinion of the physician exercising competent medical judgment, the child has no reasonable chance of recovery from a terminal illness.
**Privileged Communications:** the privileged quality of communication between husband and wife and any professional person and his or her patient or client, except that between attorney and client, is hereby abrogated in situations involving known or suspected child abuse or neglect and shall not constitute grounds for failure to report, failure to cooperate with the department in its activities, or failure to give or accept evidence in any judicial proceeding relating to child abuse or neglect.

**Procedures:** R.I. Gen. Laws § 40-11-3 (a) (2008); § 40-11-6 (2008)
**Individual Responsibility:** any person who has reasonable cause to know or suspect that any child has been abused or neglected shall, within 24 hours, transfer that information to the Dept. for Children and Their Families or its agent who shall cause the report to be investigated immediately.

The Dept. of Children and Their Families shall establish and implement a single, statewide, toll-free telephone to operate 24 hours per day, seven days per week for the receipt of reports concerning child abuse and neglect, which reports shall be electronically recorded and placed in the central registry.

When any physician or duly certified registered nurse practitioner has cause to suspect that a child brought to him or her for examination, care, or treatment is an abused or neglected child, or when the child is under the age of 12 and is suffering from any sexually transmitted disease, he or she shall report the incident or cause a report to be made immediately, by telephone or otherwise, to both the department and the law enforcement agency, and shall be followed by a report in writing explaining the extent and nature of the abuse or neglect the child is alleged to have suffered.

**Immunity:** R.I. Gen. Laws § 40-11-4 (2008)
A person participating in good faith in making a report pursuant to the reporting laws shall have immunity from any civil or criminal liability that might otherwise be incurred or imposed. Any such participant shall have the same immunity with respect to participation in any judicial proceeding resulting from the report.

**Failure to Report:** R.I. Gen. Laws § 40-11-6.1 (2008)
Any person, official, physician, or institution required by law to report known or suspected child abuse or neglect or to perform any other act who knowingly fails to do so or who knowingly prevents any person acting reasonably from doing so shall be guilty of a misdemeanor, and upon conviction thereof, shall be subject to a fine of not more than $500 or imprisonment for not more than one year, or both.

In addition, any person, official, physician, or institution who knowingly fails to perform any act required by the reporting laws or who knowingly prevents another person from performing a required act shall be civilly liable for the damages proximately caused by that failure.

**False Reporting:** R.I. Gen. Laws § 40-11-3.2 (2008)
Any person who knowingly and willingly makes or causes to be made to the Department a false report of child abuse or neglect shall be guilty of a misdemeanor and, upon conviction thereof, shall be fined not more than $1,000 or imprisoned not more than one year, or both.

# SOUTH CAROLINA

**Definitions:** S.C. CODE ANN. § 20-7-490 (2008)
**Child Abuse or Neglect:** occurs when the parent, guardian, or other person responsible for the child's welfare:

(a) inflicts or allows to be inflicted upon the child physical or mental injury or engages in acts or omissions which present a substantial risk of physical or mental injury to the child, including injuries sustained as a result of excessive corporal punishment, but excluding corporal punishment or physical discipline which:
    (i) is administered by a parent or person in loco parentis;
    (ii) is perpetrated for the sole purpose of restraining or correcting the child;
    (iii) is reasonable in manner and moderate in degree;
    (iv) has not brought about permanent or lasting damage to the child; and
    (v) is not reckless or grossly negligent behavior by the parents.

(b) commits or allows to be committed against the child a sexual offense as defined by the laws of this State or engages in acts or omissions that present a substantial risk that a sexual offense as defined in the laws of this State would be committed against the child;

(c) fails to supply the child with adequate food, clothing, shelter, or education as required under Article 1 of Chapter 65 of Title 59, supervision appropriate to the child's age and development, or health care though financially able to do so or offered financial or other reasonable means to do so and the failure to do so has caused or presents a substantial risk of causing physical or mental injury. However, a child's absences from school may not be considered abuse or neglect unless the school has made efforts to bring about the child's attendance, and those efforts were unsuccessful because of the parents' refusal to cooperate. For the purpose of this chapter "adequate health care" includes any medical or nonmedical remedial health care permitted or authorized under state law;

(d) abandons the child;

(e) encourages, condones, or approves the commission of delinquent acts by the child and the commission of the acts are shown to be the result of the encouragement, condonation, or approval; or

(f) has committed abuse or neglect as described in subsections (a) through (e) such that a child who subsequently becomes part of the person's household is at substantial risk of one of those forms of abuse or neglect.

**Physical Injury:** death or permanent or temporary disfigurement or impairment of any bodily organ or function.

**Mental Injury:** injury to the intellectual or psychological capacity of a child as evidenced by a discernible and substantial impairment of the child's ability to function when supported by the opinion of a mental health or medical professional.

**Reporting:** S.C. CODE ANN. § 20-7-310 (2010), Code 1976 §63-7-420 (2008)
**Who Must Report:** physician, nurse, dentist, optometrist, medical examiner, or coroner, or an employee of a county medical examiner's or coroner's office, or any other medical, emergency medical services, mental health, or allied health professional, member of the clergy including a Christian Science Practitioner or religious healer, school teacher, counselor, principal, assistant principal, school attendance officer, social or public assistance worker, substance abuse treatment staff, or childcare worker in a childcare center or foster care facility, foster parent, police or law enforcement officer, juvenile justice worker, undertaker, funeral home director or employee of a funeral home, persons responsible for processing films, computer technician, judge, or a volunteer non-attorney guardian ad litem serving on behalf of the South Carolina Guardian Ad Litem Program or on behalf of Richland County CASA.
**Circumstances:** when, in their professional capacity, the person has received information which gives the person reason to believe that a child's physical or mental health or welfare has been or may be adversely affected by abuse or neglect.
**Privileged Communications:** the privileged quality of communication between a husband and wife and any professional person and his patient or client, except for that between an attorney and client or a priest and penitent, is abrogated and does not constitute grounds for failure to report, or the exclusion of evidence in a civil protective proceeding resulting from a report.

**Procedures:** S.C. CODE ANN. § 20-7-310 (2010)
**Individual Responsibility:** any mandated reporter shall report in accordance with the reporting laws when in the person's professional capacity the person has received information which gives the person reason to believe that a child's physical or mental health or welfare has been or may be adversely affected by abuse or neglect.

Reports of child abuse or neglect may be made orally by telephone or otherwise to the county Dept. of Social Services or to a law enforcement agency in the county where the child resides or is found.

**Immunity:** Code 1976 §63-7-390
A person required or permitted to report pursuant to Section 63-7-310 or who participates in an investigation or judicial proceedings resulting from the report, acting in good faith, is immune from civil and criminal liability which might otherwise result by reason of these actions. In all such civil or criminal proceedings, good faith is rebuttably presumed. Immunity under this section extends to full disclosure by the person of facts which gave the person reason to believe that the child's physical or mental health or welfare had been or might be adversely affected by abuse or neglect.

**Failure to Report:** Code 1976 §63-7-410(2008)
Any person required to report a case of child abuse or neglect or any person required to perform any other function under the reporting laws who knowingly fails to do so or a person who threatens or attempts to intimidate a witness is guilty of a misdemeanor and, upon conviction, must be fined not more than $500 or be imprisoned for not more than six months, or both.

**False Reporting:** Code 1976 §63-7-430 (2008)
(A) If the family court determines pursuant to Section 63-7-2000 that a person has made a report of suspected child abuse or neglect maliciously or in bad faith or if a person has been found guilty of making a false report pursuant to Section 63-7-440, the department may bring a civil action to recover the costs of the department's investigation and proceedings associated with the investigation, including attorney's fees. The department also is entitled to recover costs and attorney's fees incurred in the civil action authorized by this section. The decision of whether to bring a civil action pursuant to this section is in the sole discretion of the department.
(B) If the family court determines pursuant to Section 63-7-2000 that a person has made a false report of suspected child abuse or neglect maliciously or in bad faith or if a person has been found guilty of making a false report pursuant to Section 63-7-440, a person who was subject of the false report has a civil cause of action against the person who made the false report and is entitled to recover from the person who made the false report such relief as may be appropriate, including:
(1) actual damages;
(2) punitive damages; and
(3) a reasonable attorney's fee and other litigation costs reasonably incurred.

## SOUTH DAKOTA

**Definitions:** S.D. CODIFIED LAWS § 26-8A-2 (2008)
**Abused and Neglected Child:** a child whose parent, guardian, or custodian has abandoned the child or has subjected the child to mistreatment or abuse; who lacks proper parental care through the actions or omissions of the child's parent, guardian, or custodian; whose environment is injurious to the child's welfare; whose parent, guardian, or custodian fails or refuses to provide proper or necessary subsistence, supervision, education, medical care, or any other care necessary for the child's health, guidance, or well-being; who is homeless, without proper care, or not domiciled with the child's parent, guardian, or custodian through no fault of the child's parent, guardian, or custodian; who is threatened with substantial harm; who has sustained emotional harm or mental injury as indicated by an injury to the child's intellectual or psychological capacity evidenced by an observable and substantial impairment in the child's ability to function within the child's normal range of performance and behavior, with due regard to the child's culture; who is subject to sexual abuse, sexual molestation, or sexual exploitation by the child's parent, guardian or custodian, or any other person responsible for the child's care; or who was subject to prenatal exposure to abusive use of alcohol or any controlled drug or substance not lawfully prescribed by a practitioner as authorized by statute.

**Reporting:** S.D. Codified Laws § 26–8A-3 (2008)
**Who Must Report:** physicians; dentists; doctors or osteopathy; chiropractors; optometrists; podiatrists; hospital interns, or residents; nurses; coroners; teachers; school counselors; school officials; licensed or registered child welfare providers; mental health professionals or counselors; psychologists; social workers; chemical dependency counselors; employees or volunteers of domestic abuse shelters; religious healing practitioners; parole or court service officers; law enforcement officers.
**Circumstances:** when they have reasonable cause to suspect that a child under the age of 18 has been abused or neglected.
**Privileged Communications:** the privilege of confidentiality set forth in statutes regarding physician–patient privilege, husband–wife privilege, school counselor–student privilege, and social worker–client privilege may not be claimed in any judicial proceeding involving an alleged abused or neglected child or resulting from the giving or causing the giving of a report concerning abuse or neglect of a child pursuant to the reporting laws.

**Procedures:** S.D. Codified Laws § 26–8A-6, -7, -8, -10 (2008)
**Individual Responsibility:** the reports required from mandated reporters shall be made orally and immediately by telephone or otherwise to the state's attorney of the county in which the child resides or is present, to the Dept. of Social Services or to law enforcement officers.

Any person who has contact with a child as a member of a staff of a hospital or similar institution shall immediately notify the person in charge or his designee of suspected abuse or neglect. The person in charge shall report the information in accordance with law. Any person required to report shall also promptly submit to the state's attorney complete copies of medical examination, treatment and hospital records regarding the child.

Any person who has contact with a child in any public or private school, whether accredited or unaccredited, as a teacher, nurse, counselor, official or administrator, or any person providing services pursuant to law shall notify the school superintendent or principal or designee of suspected abuse or neglect. The person in charge shall report the information in accordance with law.
**Content of Report:** a report shall include the name, address, date and place of birth of the child; the name and address of the child's parents, guardian, custodian, or responsible persons; the date of the report; and the suspected or proven instances of child abuse or neglect.

**Immunity:** S.D. Codified Laws § 26–8A-14 (2008)
Any person or party participating in good faith in the making of a report or the submitting of copies of medical examination, treatment or hospitalization records pursuant to the reporting laws, is immune from any civil or criminal liability that might otherwise be incurred or imposed, and has the same immunity for participation in any judicial proceeding resulting from the report.

Immunity also extends in the same manner to persons requesting the taking of photographs and x-rays pursuant to the reporting laws, to persons taking the photographs and x-rays, to child protection teams established by the Secretary of Social Services, to public officials or employees involved in the investigation and treatment of child abuse or neglect, or to any person who in good faith cooperates with a child protection team or the Dept. of Social Services in investigation, placement, or a treatment plan.

The provisions of this law or any other law granting or allowing the grant of immunity do not extend to any person alleged to have committed an act or acts of child abuse or neglect.

**Failure to Report:** S.D. Codified Laws § 26–8A-4, -6, -7 (2008); § 26–8A-3 (2008)
Any person who intentionally fails to make the required report is guilty of a Class 1 misdemeanor.
Any person who knowingly and intentionally fails to make a report is guilty of a Class 1 misdemeanor.

Any staff member of a hospital or similar institution who knowingly and intentionally fails to make a required report and to submit copies of records is guilty of a Class 1 misdemeanor. Each hospital or similar institution shall have a written policy on reporting of child abuse and neglect and submission of copies of medical examination, treatment, and hospital records to the state's attorney.

Any staff member of a public or private school who knowingly and intentionally fails to make a required report is guilty of a Class 1 misdemeanor. Each school district shall have a written policy on reporting of child abuse and neglect.

Required to report a case of child abuse or neglect or any person required to perform any other function under the reporting laws, who knowingly fails to do so, or a person who threatens or attempts to intimidate a witness, is guilty of a misdemeanor and, upon conviction, must be fined not more than $500 or be imprisoned for not more than six months, or both.

**False Reporting:**
Not specifically addressed in statute.

# TENNESSEE

**Definitions:** TENN. CODE ANN. § 37-1-401, -602 (a) (2008)
**Child:** a person who is, or is reasonably presumed to be, under 18.
**Child Sexual Abuse:** the commission of any act involving unlawful sexual abuse, molestation, fondling or carnal knowledge of a child under 13 that on or after November 1, 1989, constituted the criminal offenses of aggravated rape; rape; aggravated sexual battery; sexual battery; criminal attempt for any of the offenses listed above; incest; sexual exploitation of a minor; aggravated sexual exploitation of a minor; especially aggravated sexual exploitation of a minor. Also, means the commission of any act specified above against a child 13 through 17 if act is committed against the child by a parent, guardian, relative, person residing in the child's home, or other responsible person. (Statute also provides list of specific acts considered to be sexual abuse.)
**Mental Injury:** an injury to the intellectual or psychological capacity of a child as evidenced by a discernible and substantial impairment in the child's ability to function in the child's normal range of performance, with due regard to the child's culture.

**Reporting:** TENN. CODE ANN. § 37-1-403, -605 (a), -411 (2010)
**Who Must Report:** Any person who has knowledge of or is called upon to render aid to any child who is suffering from or has sustained any wound, injury, disability, or physical or mental condition shall report.
**Circumstances:** when they have knowledge of or are called upon to render aid to any child who is suffering from or has sustained any would, injury, disability, or physical or mental condition which is of such a nature as to reasonably indicate that it has been caused by brutality, abuse, or neglect; or on the basis of available information, reasonably appears to have been caused by brutality, abuse, or neglect; when they know or have reasonable cause to suspect that a child has been sexually abused.
**Privileged Communications:** neither the husband–wife privilege nor psychiatrist–patient privilege nor the psychologist–patient privilege is a ground for excluding evidence regarding harm or the cause of harm to a child in any dependency and neglect proceeding resulting from a report of harm or a prosecution for severe child abuse.

**Procedures:** TENN. CODE ANN. § 37-1-403 (a)-(d), -605 (a) (2008)
**Individual Responsibility:** any mandated reporter shall report such harm immediately, by telephone or otherwise, to the judge having juvenile jurisdiction or to the county office of the Dept. of Children's Services or to the office of the sheriff or the chief law enforcement official or the municipality where the child resides. Any mandated reporter who knows or has reasonable cause to suspect that a child has been sexually abused shall report such knowledge or suspicion to the Dept. of Children's services in the manner prescribed by law.

If a hospital, clinic, school or any other organization responsible for the care of children has a specific procedure, approved by the director of the county office of the Dept. of Children's Services, any member of its staff whose duty to report as a member of the staff of the organization may fulfill that duty by reporting instead to the person in charge of the organization or such person's designee who shall make the report in accordance to law.

**Content of Report:** the report shall include, to the extent known by the reporter: the name, address, and age of the child; the name and address of the person responsible for the care of the child; the facts requiring the report; the report may include any other pertinent information.

**Immunity:** Tenn. Code Ann. § 37-1-410 (a) (2010)
If a health care provider makes a required report in good faith, he/she shall not be liable in a civil or criminal action based upon the decision to report.
(B) Because of the overriding public policy to encourage all persons to report the neglect of or harm or abuse to children, any person upon whom good faith immunity is conferred pursuant to this subdivision
(a)(5) shall be presumed to have acted in good faith in making a report of harm.
(6) No immunity conferred pursuant to this subsection (a) shall attach if the person reporting the harm perpetrated or inflicted the abuse or caused the neglect.
(7) A person furnishing a report, information or records as required, requested, or authorized under this part shall have the same immunity and the same scope of immunity with respect to testimony such person may be required to give or may give in any judicial or administrative proceeding or in any communications with the department or any law enforcement official as is otherwise conferred by this subsection (a) upon the person for making the report of harm.
(8) If the person furnishing a report, information or records during the normal course of the person's duties as required or authorized or requested under this part is different from the person originally reporting the harm, then the person furnishing the report, information or records shall have the same immunity and the same scope of immunity with respect to testimony the person may be required to give or may give in any judicial or administrative proceeding or in any communications with the department or any law enforcement official as is otherwise conferred by this subsection (a) upon the person who made the original report of harm.
(b) Any person reporting under this part shall have a civil cause of action against any person who causes a detrimental change in the employment status of the reporting party by reason of the report.

**Failure to Report:** Tenn. Code Ann. § 37-1-412 (a) (2008)
Any person who knowingly fails to make a report required by the reporting laws commits a Class A misdemeanor.

**False Reporting:** Tenn. Code Ann. § 37-1-413 (2008)
Any person who either verbally or by written or printed communication knowingly and maliciously reports, or causes, encourages, aids, counsels, or procures another to report a false accusation of child sexual abuse commits a Class E felony.

# TEXAS

**Definitions:** Tex. Fam. Code Ann. § 261.001 (2007)
**Abuse:** the following acts or omissions: causing or permitting mental/emotional injury causing observable/material impairment in a child's development or psychological functioning; physical injury that results in harm or genuine threat, including injury at variance with the explanation given (excluding an accident/reasonable discipline); failure to reasonably prevent another person to injure or harm a child; sexual conduct harmful to a child's mental, emotional, or physical welfare; failure to reasonably prevent sexual conduct (Penal Code 43.01- sexual contact/intercourse, deviate sexual intercourse); causing or allowing the depicting of a child for the purpose of obscenity or pornography; the current use of a controlled substance in a manner/extent that it injures a child; or causing or encouraging a child to use a controlled substance.
**Neglect:** the leaving of a child which causes a substantial risk of physical or mental harm without arranging for necessary care and showing an intent not to return; placing a child in or failing to remove a child from a situation beyond the child's level of maturity, physical condition, or mental abilities that results in injury or a substantial risk of immediate harm; failing to seek medical care for a child, with the failure causing a substantial risk of death, disfigurement, or injury; failure to provide necessary food, clothing, or shelter; allowing or exposing a child to a substantial risk of harmful sexual conduct.

**Reporting:** Tex. Fam. Code Ann. § 261.101 (a)-(c) (2005); § 261.102 (2005)
**Who Must Report:** any person; professionals who in the course of their professional work have contact with children, including teachers, nurses, doctors, day-care employees, juvenile probation officers, juvenile detention or correctional officers, and employees or clinics that provide reproductive services.
**Circumstances:** when they have cause to believe that a child has been or may be abused or neglected or has died of abuse or neglect.
**Privileged Communications:** the requirement to report under this section applies without exception to an individual whose personal communications may otherwise be privileged, including an attorney, a member of the clergy, a medical practitioner, a social worker, a mental health professional, and an employee of a clinic or health care facility that provides reproductive services.

**Procedures:** Tex. Fam. Code Ann. § 261.101 (2005); §§ 261.103, -.104 (2005)
**Individual Responsibility:** a person having cause to believe that a child's physical or mental health or welfare has been adversely affected by abuse or neglect by any person shall immediately make a report as provided by this subchapter. If a professional has cause to believe that a child has been or may be abused or neglected, the professional shall make a report not later than the 48th hour after the professional first suspects that the child has been or may be abused or neglected. A professional may not delegate to or rely on another person to make the report.

A report shall be made to any local or state law enforcement agency; the department if the alleged or suspected abuse involves a person responsible for the care, custody, or welfare of the child; the state agency that operates, licenses, or registers the facility in which the alleged abuse or neglect occurred; or the agency designated by the court to be responsible for the protection of children.
**Content of Report:** the person making a report shall identify, if known, the name and address of the child; the name and address of the person responsible for the care, custody, or welfare of the child; and any other pertinent information concerning the alleged or suspected abuse or neglect.

**Immunity:** Tex. Fam. Code Ann. § 261.106 (2007)
A person acting in good faith who reports or assists in the investigation of a report of alleged child abuse or neglect or who testifies or otherwise participates in a judicial proceeding arising from a report, petition, or investigation of alleged child abuse or neglect is immune from civil or criminal liability that might otherwise be incurred or imposed.

Immunity from civil and criminal liability extends to an authorized volunteer of the Dept. of Human Services or a law enforcement officer who participates at the request of the Department in an investigation of alleged or suspected abuse or neglect or in an action arising from an investigation if the person was acting in good faith and in the scope of the person's responsibilities.

A person who reports the person's own abuse or neglect of a child or who acts in bad faith or with malicious purpose in reporting alleged child abuse or neglect is not immune from civil or criminal liability.

**Failure to Report:** Tex. Fam. Code Ann. § 261.109 (2008)
A person who has cause to believe that a child's physical or mental health or welfare has been or may be adversely affected by abuse or neglect and knowingly fails to report in accordance with the reporting laws is guilty of a Class B misdemeanor.

**False Reporting:** Tex. Fam. Code Ann. § 261.107 (2008)
A person commits an offense if the person knowingly or intentionally makes a report under the reporting laws the person knows is false or lacks factual foundation. An offense under this law is felony unless it is shown at trial that the person has previously been convicted for the same offense, in which case the offense is a 3rd degree felony.

A finding by a court in a suit affecting the parent-child relationship that a report made under the reporting laws before or during the suit was false or lacking factual foundation may be grounds for the court to modify an order providing for possession of or access to the child who was the subject of the report by restricting further access to the child by the person who made the report. A person who engages in conduct described by Subsection (a) is liable to the state for a civil penalty of $1,000. The attorney general shall bring an action to recover a civil penalty authorized by this subsection.

# UTAH

**Definitions:** Utah Code Ann. § 62A-4a-101 (2009)
Child: a person under 18 years.
Abuse: means
    (i) non-accidental harm of a child;
    (ii) threatened harm of a child;
    (iii) sexual exploitation; or
    (iv) sexual abuse.
Harm: means
    (a) physical, emotional, or developmental injury or damage;
    (b) sexual abuse; or
    (c) sexual exploitation.
Incest: having sexual intercourse with a person whom the perpetrator knows to be his or her ancestor, descendant, brother, sister, uncle, aunt, nephew, niece, or first cousin, including relationships of the whole or half blood (without regard to legitimacy), adoption and stepparent and stepchild.
Molestation: touching the anus or any part of the genitals of a child or taking indecent liberties with the intent to arouse or gratify the sexual desire of any person.
Sexual Abuse: acts or attempted acts of intercourse, sodomy, or molestation directed to a child.
Sexual Exploitation of Minors: means knowingly:
    (a) employing, using, persuading, inducing, enticing, or coercing any child to:
      (i) pose in the nude for the purpose of sexual arousal of any person; or
      (ii) engage in any sexual or simulated sexual conduct for the purpose of photographing, filming, recording, or displaying in any way the sexual or simulated sexual conduct;
    (b) displaying, distributing, possessing for the purpose of distribution, or selling material depicting a child:
      (i) in the nude, for the purpose of sexual arousal of any person; or
      (ii) engaging in sexual or simulated sexual conduct; or
    (c) engaging in any conduct that would constitute an offense under law, regardless of whether the person who engages in the conduct is actually charged with, or convicted of, the offense.

**Reporting:** Utah Code Ann. § 62A-4a-403 (1)- (3) (2008); § 62A-4a-412 (2008)
Who Must Report: persons licensed under the Medical Practice Act or the Nurse Practice Act; any persons.
Circumstances: when they have reason to believe that a child has been subjected to incest, molestation, sexual exploitation, sexual abuse, physical abuse, or neglect; when they observe a child being subjected to conditions or circumstances which reasonably result in sexual abuse, physical abuse, or neglect.
Privileged Communications: the reporting requirements do not apply to a clergyman or priest, without consent of the person making the confession, with regard to any confession made to him in his professional character if the confession was made directly to the clergyman or priest by the perpetrator; and the clergyman or priest is, under canon law or church doctrine or practice, bound to maintain the confidentiality of that confession. When receiving information from any other source, he is required to give notification on the basis of that information even though he may have received the same information from the confession. Exemption from reporting does not exempt a clergyman or priest from any other efforts to prevent further abuse or neglect.
    The physician–patient privilege is not a ground for excluding evidence regarding a child's injuries or the cause of those injuries, in any proceeding resulting from a report made in good faith pursuant to reporting.

**Procedures:** Utah Code Ann. § 62A-4a-403, -408 (2008)
Individual Responsibility: when a mandated reporter has reason to believe that a child has been subjected to incest, molestation, sexual exploitation, sexual abuse, physical abuse, or neglect or who observes a child being subjected to conditions or circumstances which would reasonably result in sexual abuse, physical abuse, or neglect, he or she shall immediately notify the nearest peace officer, law enforcement agency, or office of the Division of Child and Family Services.
    Reports made pursuant to this part shall be followed by a written report within 48 hours, if requested by the Division of Child and Family Services.

**Immunity:** UTAH CODE ANN. § 62A-4a-410 (2008)
Any person, official, or institution participating in good faith in making a report, taking photographs or x-rays, assisting an investigator from the division, serving as a member of a child protection team, or taking a child into protective custody pursuant to the reporting laws is immune from any civil or criminal liability that otherwise might result by reason of those actions.

**Failure to Report:** UTAH CODE ANN. § 62A-4a-411 (2008)
Any person, official, or institution required to report a case of suspected child abuse, child sexual abuse, neglect, fetal alcohol syndrome, or fetal drug dependency who willfully fails to do so is guilty of a Class B misdemeanor. Action for failure to report must be commenced within four years from the date of knowledge of the offense and the willful failure to report.

**False Reporting:**
Not specifically addressed in statute.

# VERMONT

**Definitions:** VT. STAT. ANN. tit. 33, § 4912 (2008)
**Abused or Neglected Child:** a child whose physical health; psychological growth and development, or welfare is harmed or is at substantial risk of harm by the acts or omissions of his or her parent or other person responsible for the child's welfare; or a child who is sexually abused or at substantial risk of sexual abuse by any person.
**Child:** an individual under the age of majority.
**Emotional Maltreatment:** a pattern of malicious behavior which results in impaired psychological growth and development.
**Physical Injury:** death or permanent or temporary disfigurement or impairment of any bodily organ or function by other than accidental means.
**Sexual Abuse:** consists of any act or acts by any person involving sexual molestation or exploitation of a child, including but not limited to, incest, prostitution, rape, sodomy, or any lewd and lascivious conduct involving a child; also includes the aiding, abetting, counseling, hiring, or procuring of a child to perform or participate in any photograph, motion picture, exhibition, show, representation, or other presentation which, in whole or in part, depicts sexual conduct, sexual excitement, or sadomasochistic abuse involving a child.

**Reporting:** VT. STAT. ANN. tit. 33, § 4913 (2007)
**Who Must Report:** physicians, surgeons, osteopaths, chiropractors, physician's assistants, resident physicians, interns, or hospital administrators in any hospital in this state, whether not so registered, and registered nurses, licensed practical nurses, medical examiners, dentists, psychologists, or other health care providers; school superintendents, school teachers, school librarians, day care workers, school principals, school guidance counselors, mental health professionals, or social workers; probation officers, police officers, camp owners, camp administrators or camp counselors. As used in this subsection, "camp" includes any residential or nonresidential recreational program.
**Circumstances:** when they have reasonable cause to believe that any child has been abused or neglected.

**Procedures:** VT. STAT. ANN. tit. 33, § 4914 (2007); § 4913 (a) (2007)
**Individual Responsibility:** any mandatory reporter shall report or cause a report to be made in accordance with the provisions of section 4914 concerning content of report within 24 hours.
**Content of Report:** reports shall contain the name and address of the reporter; the names and addresses of the child and the parents or other persons responsible for the child's care, if known; the age of the child; the nature and extent of the child's injuries; any evidence of previous abuse and neglect of the child or the child's siblings; any other information that the reporter believes might be helpful in establishing the cause of the injuries, establishing the reasons for neglect, protecting the child, and assisting the family.

**Immunity:** VT. STAT. ANN. tit. 33, § 4913 (d) (2007)
Any person enumerated in subsections (a) or (b) of this section, other than a person suspected of child abuse, who in good faith makes a report to the Department of Social and Rehabilitation Services shall be immune from any civil or criminal liability which might otherwise be incurred or imposed as a result of making a report.

**Failure to Report:** VT. STAT. ANN. tit. 33, § 4913 (f) (2009)
Any person who violates the reporting laws shall be fined not more than $500 unless they did so with an intent to conceal abuse or neglect, in which case, that person shall be imprisoned for not more than 6 months and fined not more than $1000.

**False Reporting:**
Not specifically addressed in statute.

# VIRGINIA

**Definitions:** VA. CODE. ANN. § 63.2–100 (2009)
**Abused or Neglected Child:** any child less than 18 years of age whose parents or other persons responsible for his or her care creates or inflicts, threatens to create or inflict, or allows to be created or inflicted upon such child a physical or mental injury by other than accidental means, or creates a substantial risk of death, disfigurement, or impairment, or impairment of bodily or mental functions; whose parents or other person responsible for his care neglects or refuses to provide care necessary for his health; whose parents or other person responsible for his care abandons such child; whose parents or other person responsible for his care commits or allows to be committed any act of sexual exploitation or any sexual act upon a child in violation of the law; or who is without parental care or guardianship caused by the unreasonable absence or the mental or physical incapacity of the child's parent, guardian, legal custodian, or other person standing in loco parentis.

**Reporting:** VA. CODE. ANN. § 63.2–1509 (2009)
**Who Must Report:** persons licensed to practice medicine or any of the healing arts; hospital residents or interns; persons employed in the nursing profession; other professional staff persons employed by hospitals, institutions, or facilities to which children have been committed or placed for care and treatment; duly accredited Christian Science practitioners; teachers or other persons employed in public or private schools, kindergartens, or nursery schools; persons providing child care for pay on a regularly planned basis; persons employed as social workers; mental health professionals; any persons associated with or employed by private organizations responsible for the care, custody, and control of children; probation officers; law enforcement officers; mediators eligible to receive court referrals.
**Circumstances:** when they have reason to suspect that a child is an abused or neglected child.

**Procedures:** VA. CODE. ANN. § 63.2–1509 (2009)
**Individual Responsibility:** mandatory reporters shall report the matter immediately, except as hereinafter provided, to the local department of the county or city wherein the child resides or wherein the abuse or neglect is believed to have occurred or to the Dept. of Social Services' toll-free child abuse and neglect hotline.

If the information is received by a teacher, staff member, resident, intern or nurse in the course of professional services in a hospital, school, or similar institution, such person, may, in place of said report, immediately notify the person in charge of the institution or department, or his designee, who shall make such report forthwith.

If an employee of the local department is suspected of abusing or neglecting a child, the report shall be made to the juvenile and domestic relations district court of the county or city where the abuse or neglect was discovered.
**Content of Report:** the initial report may be an oral report, but such report shall be reduced to writing by the child abuse coordinator of the local department. The person required to make the report shall disclose all information which is the basis for his or her suspicion of abuse or neglect of the child and, upon request, shall make available to the coordinator or local department any records or reports which document the basis for the report.

**Immunity:** VA. CODE. ANN. § 63.2–1512 (2009)
Any person who makes a report or complaint pursuant to the reporting laws or who takes a child into custody pursuant to law or who participates in a judicial proceeding resulting from such actions shall be immune from any civil or criminal liability in connection therewith, unless it is proven that such person acted in bad faith or with malicious intent.

**Failure to Report:** VA. CODE. ANN. § 63.2-1509 (2009)
Any person required to file a report pursuant to the reporting laws who fails to do so within 72 hours of his first suspicion of child abuse or neglect shall be fined not more than $500 for the first failure and for any subsequent failures not less than $100 nor more than $1,000.

**False Reporting:** VA. CODE. ANN. § 63.2-1513 (2009)
Any person 14 years of age or older who makes or causes to be made a report of child abuse or neglect which he knows to be false shall be guilty of a Class 1 misdemeanor.
Any person 14 years of age or older who has been previously convicted under the subsection and who is subsequently convicted of making a false report of child abuse or neglect shall be guilty of a Class 6 felony.

# WASHINGTON

**Definitions:** WASH. REV. CODE. ANN. § 26.44.020 (2007)
**Abuse or Neglect:** the injury, sexual abuse, sexual exploitation, negligent treatment, or maltreatment of a child, adult dependent, or developmentally disabled person under circumstances which indicate that the child's or adult's health, welfare, and safety is harmed, excluding conduct permitted under law.
**Child or Children:** any person under the age of 18 years.
**Negligent Treatment or Maltreatment:** an act or omission which evidences a serious disregard of consequences of such magnitude as to constitute a clear and present danger to the child's health, welfare, and safety. Siblings sharing a bedroom is not "negligent treatment or maltreatment."
**Severe Abuse:** any single act of abuse that causes physical trauma of sufficient severity that, if left untreated, could cause death; any single act of sexual abuse that causes significant bleeding, deep bruising, or significant external or internal swelling; or more than one act of physical abuse, each of which causes bleeding, deep bruising, significant external or internal swelling, bone fracture, or unconsciousness.
**Sexual Exploitation:** includes allowing or encouraging a child to engage in prostitution; or allowing, permitting, encouraging or engaging in the obscene or pornographic photographing, filming or depicting of a child.

**Reporting:** WASH. REV. CODE. ANN. § 26.44.030 (2007)
**Who Must Report:** practitioners; county coroners or medical examiners; pharmacists; registered or licensed nurses; professional school personnel; licensed or certified child care providers or their employees; social service counselors; psychologists; employees of the State Dept. of Social and Health Services; juvenile probation officers; law enforcement officers; personnel of the Dept. of Corrections; persons who process or produce visual or printed matter; any other adult.
**Circumstances:** when they have reasonable cause to believe that a child or adult dependent or developmentally disabled person has suffered abuse or neglect.
The reporting requirement does not apply to the discovery of abuse or neglect that occurred during childhood if it is discovered after the child has become an adult. However, if there is reasonable cause to believe other children, dependent adults, or developmentally disabled persons are or may be at risk of abuse or neglect by the accused, the reporting requirements shall apply.
**Privileged Communications:** conduct conforming with the reporting requirements shall not be deemed a violation of the confidentiality privilege of §§ 5.60.060 (clergy and physician privileges), 18.53.200 (optometrist privilege), and 18.83.110 (psychologist privilege).

**Procedures:** Wash. Rev. Code. Ann. § 26.44.030 (2007); § 26.44.040 (2007)
**Individual Responsibility:** when any mandated reporter has reasonable cause to believe that a child or adult dependent or developmentally disabled person, has suffered abuse or neglect, he or she shall report such incident, or cause a report to be made, to the proper law enforcement agency or to the Department as provided in § 26.44.040.

The report shall be made at the first opportunity, but in no case longer than 48 hours after there is reasonable cause to believe that the child or adult has suffered abuse or neglect. The report shall include the identity of the accused if known.

**Content of Report:** an immediate oral report shall be made by telephone or otherwise to the proper law enforcement agency or the Dept. of Social and Health Services and, upon request, shall be followed by a report in writing. Reports shall contain the following, if known: the name, address, and age of child, adult dependent or developmentally disabled person; the name and address of the child's parents, stepparents, guardians, or other persons having custody of the child, adult dependent or developmentally disabled person; the nature and extent of the alleged injury or injuries, alleged neglect, or alleged sexual abuse; any evidence of previous injuries, including their nature and extent; and any other information which may be helpful in establishing the cause of death, injury, or injuries and the identity of the alleged perpetrator or perpetrators.

**Immunity:** Wash. Rev. Code. Ann. § 26.44.060 (1)(a) (2007)
Any person participating in good faith in the making of a report pursuant to the reporting laws or testifying as to alleged child abuse or neglect in a judicial proceeding shall be immune from any liability arising out of such reporting or testifying.

**Failure to Report:** Wash. Rev. Code. Ann. § 26.44.080 (2007)
Every person who is required to make, or to cause to be made, a report pursuant to the reporting laws and who knowingly fails to make or fails to cause such report to be made shall be guilty of a gross misdemeanor.

**False Reporting:** Wash. Rev. Code. Ann. § 26.44.060 (4) (2007)
A person who, intentionally and in bad faith or maliciously, knowingly makes a false report of abuse or neglect shall be guilty of a misdemeanor punishable in accordance with the law.

# WEST VIRGINIA

**Definitions:** W. Va. Code § 49–1-3 (2011)
**Abused Child:** means a child whose health or welfare is harmed or threatened by:
(A) A parent, guardian or custodian who knowingly or intentionally inflicts, attempts to inflict or knowingly allows another person to inflict, physical injury or mental or emotional injury, upon the child or another child in the home; or
(B) Sexual abuse or sexual exploitation; or
(C) The sale or attempted sale of a child by a parent, guardian or custodian in violation of section sixteen, article four, chapter forty-eight of this code; or
(D) Domestic violence as defined in section two hundred two, article twenty-seven, chapter forty-eight of this code.
In addition to its broader meaning, physical injury may include an injury to the child as a result of excessive corporal punishment.

**Neglected Child:** means a child:
(i) Whose physical or mental health is harmed or threatened by a present refusal, failure or inability of the child's parent, guardian or custodian to supply the child with necessary food, clothing, shelter, supervision, medical care or education, when such refusal, failure or inability is not due primarily to a lack of financial means on the part of the parent, guardian or custodian; or
(ii) Who is presently without necessary food, clothing, shelter, medical care, education or supervision because of the disappearance or absence of the child's parent or custodian.

**Sexual Abuse:** means:
(A) As to a child who is less than sixteen years of age, any of the following acts which a parent, guardian or custodian shall engage in, attempt to engage in, or knowingly procure another person to engage in, with such child, notwithstanding the fact that the child may have willingly participated in such conduct or the fact that the child may have suffered no apparent physical injury or mental or emotional injury as a result of such conduct:
(i) Sexual intercourse;
(ii) Sexual intrusion; or
(iii) Sexual contact.

**Severe Physical Abuse:** bodily injury that creates a substantial risk of prolonged disfigurement, death, or loss or impairment of the function of any bodily organ.

**Reporting:** W. Va. Code § 49–6A-2, -7 (2006)
**Who Must Report:** medical, dental, or mental health professional; emergency medical services personnel; school teachers or other school personnel; child care workers or foster care workers; Christian Science practitioners; religious healers; social services workers; peace officers or law enforcement officials; members of the clergy; circuit court judges; family law masters or magistrates.
**Circumstances:** when they have reasonable cause to suspect that a child is neglected or abused; when they observe the child being subjected to conditions that are likely to result in abuse or neglect; when they believe that a child has suffered serious physical abuse or sexual assault.
**Privileged Communications:** the privileged quality of communications between husband and wife and between any professional person and his or her patient or client, except that between attorney and client, is hereby abrogated in situations involving suspected or known child abuse or neglect.

**Procedures:** W.Va. Code § 49–6A-2, -5 (2003)
**Individual Responsibility:** when any mandated reporter has reasonable cause to suspect that a child is neglected or abused or observes the child being subjected to conditions that are likely to result in abuse or neglect, such person shall immediately, and not more than 48 hours after suspecting this abuse, report the circumstances or cause a report to be made to the state Dept. of Human Services.

In any case where the reporter believes that the child suffered serious physical abuse or sexual abuse or sexual assault, the reporter shall also immediately report or cause a report to be made to the Division of Public Safety and any law enforcement agency having jurisdiction to investigate the complaint.

Any person required to report under this article who is a member of the staff of a public or private institution, school, facility, or agency shall immediately notify the person in charge of such institution, school, facility, or agency or a designated agent thereof, who shall report or cause a report to be made. Nothing in this article is intended to prevent individuals form reporting on their own behalf.

Reports of abuse and neglect shall be followed by a written report within 48 hours if so requested. The state Dept. of Human Services shall establish and maintain a 24-hour, 7-day-a-week telephone number to receive such calls reporting suspected child abuse or neglect.

Appendix A

**Immunity:** W. Va. Code § 49-6A-6 (2006)
Any person, official, or institution participating in good faith in any act permitted or required by the reporting laws shall be immune from any civil or criminal liability that otherwise might result by reason of such actions.

**Failure to Report:** W. Va. Code § 49-6A-8 (2008)
Any person, official, or institution required by law to report a case involving a child known or suspected to be abused or neglected, or required by law to forward a copy of a report of serious injury, who knowingly fails to do so, or knowingly prevents another person acting reasonably from doing so, shall be guilty of a misdemeanor, and upon conviction thereof, shall be confined in the county jail not more than 10 days or fined not more than $100, or both.

**False Reporting:**
Not specifically addressed in statute.

# WISCONSIN

**Definitions:** Wis. Stat. Ann. § 48.02 (1), (2), (5j) 2011); § 48.981 (1) (2008)
**Abuse:** any of the following: physical injury inflicted on a child by other than accidental means; when used in referring to an unborn child, serious physical harm inflicted on the unborn child, with risk of serious physical harm to child when born, caused by the habitual lack of self-control of the expectant mother in the use of alcohol, controlled substances, or analogs, exhibited to a severe degree; sexual intercourse/contact; a violation of statutes regarding sexual exploitation, child viewing or listening to sexual activity, or exposure of the genitals to a child; permitting, allowing, or encouraging a child to engage in prostitution; emotional damage which has been neglected, untreated, or un ameliorated for reasons other than poverty.
**Child:** a person who is less than 18 for purposes of this chapter.
**Emotional Damage:** harm to a child's psychological or intellectual functioning, evidenced, when exhibited in a severe degree, by depression; anxiety; withdrawal; aggressive behavior; substantial behavior change, emotional response, or cognition not within normal range.
**Neglect:** failure, refusal, or inability, for reasons other than poverty, to provide necessary care, food, clothing, medical or dental care, or shelter so as to seriously endanger the physical health of the child.

**Reporting:** Wis. Stat. Ann. § 48.981 (2), (2m)(c), (2m)(d) (2008)
**Who Must Report:** physicians; coroners; medical examiners; nurses; dentists; chiropractors; optometrists; acupuncturists; other medical professionals; physical therapists; dietitians; occupational therapists; speech-language pathologist/audiologist; EMTs; school teachers/administrators/counselors; child care workers; daycare providers; mental health professionals; alcohol/drug counselors; county department treatment staff; marriage/family therapists; professional counselor/social workers; public assistance workers, including financial/employment planners; police/law enforcement/mediators.
**Circumstances:** when they have reasonable cause to suspect that a child seen in the course of professional duties has been abused or neglected; or threatened with abuse or neglect and suspect that it will occur.

Health care providers who provide care to a child or such persons who obtain information are not required to report sexual intercourse/contact involving a child, unless they have reasonable doubts as to the voluntariness of the child's participation or if they suspect that the sexual conduct occurred with caregiver; the child suffers from a mental deficiency that makes child incapable of understanding; the child, due to age or immaturity, is incapable of understanding the consequences/nature of activity; or unconscious or unable to communicate unwillingness; or the participant is exploiting the child.

**Procedures:** Wis. Stat. Ann. § 48.981 (2), (3)(a) (2007)
**Individual Responsibility:** any mandated reporter having reasonable cause to suspect that a child seen in the course of professional duties has been abused or neglected or having reason to believe that a child seen in the course of professional duties has been threatened with abuse or neglect and that abuse or neglect of the child will occur shall report as provided under the reporting laws.

A mandated reporter shall immediately inform, by telephone or personally, the county department or, in a county having a population of 500,000 or more, the department or a licensed child welfare agency under contract with the department or the sheriff or city, village or town police department of the facts and circumstances contributing to a suspicion of child abuse or neglect or of unborn child abuse or to a belief that abuse or neglect will occur.

Any person, including an attorney, having reason to suspect that an unborn child has been abused or reason to believe that an unborn child is at substantial risk of abuse may report as provided by the reporting laws.

**Immunity:** Wis. Stat. Ann. § 48.981 (4) (2008)
Any person or institution participating in good faith in the making of a report, conducting an investigation, ordering or taking photographs, or ordering or performing medical examinations of a child or an expectant mother pursuant to the reporting laws shall have immunity from any civil or criminal liability that results by reason of the action.

For the purpose of any civil or criminal proceeding, the good faith of any person reporting under this reporting law shall be presumed.

The immunity provided herein does not apply to liability for abusing or neglecting a child or for abusing an unborn child.

**Failure to Report:** Wis. Stat. Ann. § 48.981 (6) (2008)
Whoever intentionally violates the reporting laws by failure to report as required may be fined not more than $1,000 or imprisoned not more than six months, or both.

**False Reporting:**
Not specifically addressed in statute.

# WYOMING

**Definitions:** Wyo. Stat. Ann. § 14-3-202 (a)(i)-(a)(xi) (2008)
**Abuse:** means inflicting or causing physical or mental injury, harm, or imminent danger to the physical or mental health or welfare of a child other than by accidental means, including abandonment, excessive or unreasonable corporal punishment, malnutrition or substantial risk thereof by reason of intentional or unintentional neglect, and the commission or allowing the commission of a sexual offense against a child as defined by law.
**Child:** any person under the age of 18.
**Mental Injury:** an injury to the psychological capacity or emotional stability of a child as evidenced by an observable or substantial impairment in his ability to function within a normal range of performance and behavior with due regard to his culture.
**Physical Injury:** death or any harm to a child, including, but not limited to, disfigurement, impairment of any bodily organ, skin bruising, bleeding, burns, fracture of any bone, subdural hematoma, or substantial malnutrition.
**Neglect:** with respect to a child means a failure or refusal by those responsible for the child's welfare to provide adequate care, maintenance, supervision, education, or medical, surgical, or any other care necessary for the child's well-being.

**Reporting:** Wyo. Stat. Ann. § 14-3-205 (2007); § 14-3-210 (2007)
**Who Must Report:** any person.
**Circumstances:** when they know or have reasonable cause to believe or suspect that a child has been abused or neglected; when they observe any child being subjected to conditions or circumstances that would reasonably result in abuse or neglect.
**Privileged Communications:** evidence regarding a child in a judicial proceeding resulting from a report made pursuant to the reporting laws shall not be excluded on the ground that it constitutes a privileged communication: between husband and wife; claimed under provision of law other than those regarding attorney–client, physician–patient, or clergy concerning confessions received; claimed pursuant to statute regarding the confidential communication between a family violence and sexual assault advocate and victim.

**Procedures:** Wyo. Stat. Ann. § 14-3-205 (2008)
**Individual Responsibility:** any person who knows or has reasonable cause to believe or suspect that a child has been abused or neglected or who observes any child being subjected to conditions or circumstances that would reasonably result in abuse or neglect shall immediately report it to the child protective agency or local law enforcement or cause a report to be made.

If a person reporting child abuse or neglect is a member of the staff of a medical or other public or private institution, school, facility or agency, he or she shall notify the person in charge or his or her designated agent as soon as possible, who is thereupon also responsible to make the report or cause the report to be made. Nothing in this subsection is intended to relieve individuals of their obligation to report on their own behalf unless a report has already been made or will be made.

**Immunity:** Wyo. Stat. Ann. § 14-3-209 (2007)
Any person, official, institution, or agency participating in good faith in any act required or permitted by the reporting laws is immune from any civil or criminal liability that might otherwise result by reason of the action.

For the purpose of any civil or criminal proceeding, the good faith of any person, official, or institution participating in any act permitted or required by the reporting laws shall be presumed.

### Failure to Report:
Not specifically addressed in statute.

### False Reporting:
Not specifically addressed in statute.